"I am amazed by this s   the courage and dignity in an environment of violence, violation, and neglect. I feel that I have become more aware of the need to listen to my patients and show compassion to those who seem to be burdened by undisclosed hurts and problems after reading this book.

Dr. Fred Roberts, Metamora, MI

"I have known Chelsey Ann Davenport for many years, and have been privileged to walk the healing path beside her. She is one of the most resilient women I know and one of the most determined. I believe her story will inspire and encourage other survivors in their own healing journey.

Renee Rowe, LCSW, ACSW, Oxford, MI

"WOW! That doesn't even begin to explain your new book!!! I couldn't put it down. It gripped my very soul. I know the courage it took for you to write this book, that is an encouragement to me. Thank you."

Emmy Young, Dover, Maine, Women's Support Group Leader

"I know Chelsey personally and I had no idea she had been through so much! Her life is a witness to others who have experienced unbelievable violation and victimization. Chelsey has shown us that it is possible to rise above the pain of one's past and reach out to help other people who need to know that life can still be good!"

Brooke Patel, Attorney, Lynchburg, VA

"I have been there—in those same places as Chelsey. Reading her story reminded me of the little girl that loved her daddy, before I understood the evil nature of his "affection" for me. Reading this book was very healing without triggering my old hurts."

Alyssa Johnston, Women's Support Group Leader, Forest, Virginia

"Linda has managed to write Chelsey's story with dignity and grace. This book provides deep insights into the heart and soul of the child who experiences debilitating abuse and demonstrates the courage and strengths of women and men who survive it.

Dorla Hampton, Financial Administrator, Lynch Station, Virginia

"Once you begin to read this book, you will not be able to put it down until you turn the very last page."

Pam Tucker, Business Owner, Moneta, VA

The Girl Among Thorns

WHY DID SHE STAY SO LONG?

Linda Settles

Edict House Publishing Group
Lynchburg, VA

Copyright © 2010 by Linda Settles
All rights reserved

THE GIRL AMONG THORNS: WHY DID SHE STAY SO LONG? by Linda Settles
Edict House Publishing Group
400 Court Street
Lynchburg, VA 24505
www.EdictHouse.com

This book or parts thereof may not be reproduced in any form, stored in a retrieval system, or transmitted in any form by any means—electronic, mechanical, photocopy, recording, or otherwise—without prior written permission of the publisher, except as provided by United States of America copyright law.

Cover Designer: Tangent Covers

A Percentage of Proceeds From the Sale of This Book Will Be Donated to Child Debilitation Syndrome Foundation, a non-profit organization

Publisher's Cataloging-In-Publication Data
(Prepared by The Donohue Group, Inc.)

Settles, Linda.
   The girl among thorns : why did she stay so long? / Linda Settles.

   p. ; cm.

   Includes bibliographical references.
   ISBN: 978-0-9790238-6-6

1. Adult child abuse victims--Biography. 2. Adult child sexual abuse victims--Biography. 3. Child abuse--Psychological aspects. 4. Davenport, Chelsey Ann. I. Title.

RC569.5.C55 S48 2010
616.85/822/092

Dedication

I dedicate this book to all the courageous women and men who have dared to share their truths with me over the past twenty-five years. Some of you came for counseling, but many of you met me in incidental ways on the pathway to peace, the road to recovery, and recognized a fellow traveler. Your insights, encouragement, and experiences are of great value to me and to a hurting world. Keep moving on, ever upward, and never give up hope.

I dedicate this book also to the multitude of wonderful people who are striving to understand abuse survivors, those whose compassionate hearts long to love, to encourage, and to support family, friends, spouses, and yes, even strangers, whose stories both grieve and confuse them.

It is for all of you that I write this book. It is for you that I record the childhood memories of Chelsey Ann Davenport

A Note From the Author

The story you are about to read really happened to a girl by the name of Chelsey Ann Davenport. The behaviors of the participants in this story, the dialogue remembered, and the joys and sorrows experienced are depicted just as Chelsey remembers them. Many of them have been confirmed by other family members who were present when the events occurred, and by others whose stories connected with Chelsey's as life unfolded in the Davenport home.

Many people in our nation and around the world—more than you may suppose—share parts of Chelsey's story. Maybe you read the account of Elizabeth Fritzl, the woman in Austria who was hidden in her father's basement for twenty-four years, and you wonder why she didn't find a way to overpower him and escape her confinement. You may have read, also, the story of Jaycee Dugard, the eleven-year-old girl who was kidnapped by a man and his wife and forced to live in a hovel behind their house where she was repeatedly raped, bore the man's children, and remained captive for eighteen years.

How do these things occur? What are the dynamics that hold a child hostage to her abuser long after she has reached the chronological age of an adult?

We think Chelsey's story will answer some of these questions if you read between the lines. We hope it will encourage other victims to break free from their bonds and rise above the debilitation of their childhood.

Preface

You'd never know Chelsey Ann Davenport was the girl in this story. Life always has a way of changing a person, but extraordinary lives have a way of making extraordinary changes in the people who experience them.

Chelsey told me that it's hard for her to keep the timeline straight on the events in her story, and I told her that's all right. I wanted to her to tell it as she remembered it, and I believe that's just what she did.

Memory is a tricky thing. People don't choose what they'll forget or what they'll remember. It's almost as if the memories themselves choose to hide or to disclose themselves when the time is right. Chelsey told me her memories have become her friends because they help her understand who she is and how she came to be that way.

All the names have been changed in Chelsey's story to protect the identity of those who lived it with her. Everything else is just as Chelsey told it to me.

The story I'm about to tell you really happened. It happened to a girl by the name of Chelsey Ann Davenport. Chelsey would tell it herself, but something happened to make that quite impossible, so I promised her that I would tell her story, just as she told it to me.

I felt an intense need to prove my innocence. I had learned already that good girls don't lie.

Chapter 1

I hate bridges. They start on one side of a gaping hole and don't stop until they reach the other side. Sometimes the hole is dry and you can look down into a gash in the earth. The bridge looks like a bandage laid over the gash, and there is always a danger that some drunken fool will meet you halfway across and send you plunging through the rail running along its sides.

Sometimes the bridge spans a river, and that is the kind I hate the worst. A watery death seems like an awful way to go. Maybe that's just because I stared death in the face on the water more than once, but I'll get to that later.

I liked bridges at first. But that changed when I was about three. Until then, I have vague memories of walking across a bridge with my great-grandma. I remember her as tall and straight with square shoulders. Her face was square, too, and framed in waves of short, gray hair. She didn't smile a lot, but then from the stories I've heard about my great-grandma, if I'd been her I probably wouldn't have smiled much, either. They tell me she got married to a bunch of different men and none of them treated her any better than the other. By the time she got sick of 'em all, she had a whole houseful of kids and no one to help her raise 'em.

Anyway, we were right smack in the middle of that bridge when I realized that she loved Dustin more than me. How do you figure out something like that at age three? Maybe it was because she took his hand every time he offered it and didn't seem to notice mine. Or because she didn't seem to hear a word I said, while everything he said made her reach down and tousle his hair.

Don't get me wrong. I loved my big brother. He was eleven months older and my only playmate. It's just that I knew, right from the beginning, that everybody else loved him, too, and I just wished some of that love could be left over for me. Anyway, I never liked bridges much after that.

As much as I hate bridges, I love open fields, especially when they're filled with cotton-pickers. I don't think they have those anymore, but I used to watch them moving slowly along the row, paying no mind to the sharp casing as they dug the round, white boll out of it. Some of them sang while they worked, but all of them looked like their back hurt. By the time the Arkansas sun was high in the summer sky, they started looking bent, as their canvas sacks filled out, trailing behind them like long tails between the rows.

• • •

One day I was out in the front of our house, watching, when a car went by without a driver. When I got older I knew I had to be wrong about that, but at three or four years old, that is what I saw. Maybe it was because I was really short and the driver was hunched down behind the wheel, but I couldn't think about that then.

I ran as fast as I could, which couldn't have been too fast because I was bow-legged and the heavy metal braces on my legs slowed me down. If I got to going too fast, my legs would drag behind and the top part of my body would just keep going, landing me in dirt. The adults were in the house when I dashed through the door, letting the screen slam shut behind me, and started telling them what I saw. Words fell over themselves like my upper body over my bowed legs.

My excitement waned as I realized nobody believed me. I don't blame them now—everybody knows a car doesn't just go down the road by itself. I insisted that I saw it, even when my daddy started getting mad. I could always tell when Daddy's temper was rising because his face turned almost as red as his hair and his pale blue eyes seemed to squint like most people do when they look too long at the bright sun. I hated it when he got mad, because I adored the ground he walked on.

When he looked straight at me and said, "Chelsey, that's a lie," I felt like a balloon, just popped by a needle. He not only didn't believe me, but he thought I was a liar. I had to convince him of what I had seen. I grabbed his hand and pulled him toward the door.

"Please, Daddy. Come look."

In my heart—an organ that after all had only been alive for three short years—I felt an intense need to prove my innocence. I had learned already that good girls don't lie. I also knew that bad girls weren't worth much. I'm not sure how I knew that, but I'm pretty certain I had figured it out. So I simply had to get my Daddy to see the truth. He had to see that car.

I drug him out the door, heard the screen slam shut behind me, and stood beside him between the house and the cotton field. The dirt road that crawled along the side of the field was empty. Daddy shook his head and walked back into the house, leaving me standing there alone in the front yard.

I guess I realized that Daddy must be right. A car can't go down the street without a driver. I didn't know if I was crazy, or maybe a liar after all—people don't just see things that aren't real, do they?

That's the first time I knew something was wrong with me, but it wouldn't, unfortunately, be the last.

• • •

Daddy must have forgiven me because he let me work on the outhouse with him soon after that. At least, I think it was soon. It's hard to keep the timeline straight when you are only three years old. I may have turned four before he let me help him clean the outhouse. It seemed like a rare privilege to me, to be asked to carry a big yellow bucket, and hand Daddy tools every time he needed something. I think he used some sort of hose to draw the yucky stuff out through the seat holes in the wooden bench and drain it into a blue barrel. I sure hope nobody got a hankering for that shiny blue barrel and decided to take the lid off. It looked a lot like most people's burn barrels, so such a thing was possible. Whew! They would sure be sorry if they did.

An outhouse is something you don't easily forget. The smell of it is the most obvious part, but there are other memorable features as well. For one thing, it stands alone like a small house, but it is only about four feet across and six feet high. Big enough to accommodate most people, but I did hear once about a rather large woman who got real busy in the outhouse and knocked the walls down. I could imagine how she'd feel, sitting there all exposed on that skinny bench with a deep smelly hole under her. Just thinking about it made me get that slimy feeling all over again, like when I lied about the driverless car.

That is why I was so proud of Daddy when he added a real bathroom to our three-room house. I don't remember where he put it in the order of things, because our house was what some called a "shotgun" style. It was long and narrow to accommodate its tiny lot and you had to walk through one room to get into another.

You'd think, living in such a tiny house with every room connecting like that, I'd have lots of memories of my mother. But I don't. She was there all the time, but I don't remember one thing about her until I was in the first grade.

That was when I told my Grandma Kelsey that I wanted her to be my mother. I don't know if I was just trying to flatter her or if I had some more substantial reason for saying such a thing, but Grandma, who had a proper loyalty to her grown-up daughter, promptly rebuked me and told me what a fine mother I had. She was probably right, but somehow I hadn't realized it. I'm sure she was right. I never heard anything bad about Mother, but somehow I hadn't noticed any of those fine qualities either. How could I see cars without drivers when such a thing doesn't exist and yet not see my fine mother when she was right there with me most of the time?

Now I knew something was dreadfully wrong with me, but I had no way of knowing what that "something" was. If I hadn't promptly forgotten the next chapter of my young life, I might have figured it out sooner. But I did forget. I think it took all my energy over the next twenty-five years to keep that horrible memory buried, because somehow memories have a life of their own, like cadavers that aren't quite dead when they're buried. They keep clawing at the dirt, trying to get out of the grave and make their presence known.

Chapter 2

I never could figure out how my daddy and mother came to be together. Daddy was eight years older than mother and not exactly handsome. Standing about five-feet-ten, thin except for a slight belly that grew along with his years, Daddy had squinty eyes and the ruddy complexion that commonly goes along with red hair. Mother was a beauty. She had an olive complexion and the brown eyes of a young doe. She was always a bit overweight, but even that didn't rob her of the good looks handed out by her Dutch-Irish-Indian heritage. When mother was happy, her eyes seemed to twinkle like stars—but when she was mad, they flashed, like flames of fire. I got burned lots of times by Mother's flashing eyes and frozen to death by my father's icy blue ones. I don't know which hurt the worst—the fire or the ice.

I've heard that Mother and Daddy met in the blueberry field when mother was eighteen and he was twenty-six. By the time Mother was nineteen, they were married. My daddy claimed she married him to get out of tending her younger siblings and try to get a life of her own. He said she didn't want to marry him at first, but her Grandma Abby, Mother's part-Cherokee, hunch-backed grandmother, talked her into it. Grandma Abby may have stood only five-feet tall, but she had a real way with words that just about always got her what she wanted.

Daddy said Grandma Abby told Mother she'd never do any better and she'd better grab the chance to get married while she could. That story always amazed me because I thought my beautiful mother could have married anyone she pleased.

Chapter 3

Did you ever notice how happiness is like a big squirt gun? It just sits there with nothing coming out of it, like it might as well be empty. No matter how hard the sun shines or how hot you get, all that cool refreshing water is locked away in a plastic casing and it doesn't do you any good. And then suddenly, when you least expect it, life pulls the trigger and catches you square in the face.

Those occasional squirts of happiness can keep a child alive during the dog days of summer. Watching the sun shimmer like gold dust over the parched cotton fields had a way of triggering a little squirt of happiness for me, so I think I must have missed it when my family decided to pull up stakes. We moved to Arizona because Grandma Betsy, my daddy's mother, had asthma and Arizona was supposed to cure it.

I've heard the Davenports put on quite a show during the long, long drive to Arizona. It's a wonder we made it all the way to Phoenix, since our family hadn't traveled often. I don't think the state highways were much of a challenge for my daddy, but he wasn't used to the new freeway, and the monotony of driving on it made him tired. Being country folk, he and my step-grandpa, Donny, who was following right behind him, figured the side of the road was as good as any for a few hours sleep. Just across the Arkansas-Texas state lines, they pulled both vehicles and the trailer Daddy was pulling behind him over to the nice paved shoulder and went straight to sleep.

When they woke up the next morning, they were amazed to see cars whizzing around them, and they realized we had spent the night, not on the shoulder as we supposed, but on the right lane of the freeway.

Somehow, we made it to Arizona and got ready to make a new life for ourselves. Since we didn't have much money, we got a place to stay in an abandoned army barracks. I heard it was the cheapest way to get a roof over our heads—probably because it was nothing more than a corrugated metal igloo with a concrete floor. We didn't need heat out there in the desert and there certainly wasn't any air conditioning.

Mother had already produced another brother for me, and now she was pregnant again. Somehow she managed to get pneumonia and end up in the hospital. O'dell, the third boy born into the Davenport family, was a "blue baby." That's what they called it when an infant couldn't get enough oxygen and it showed up in his face. It seems everything about that hospital stay was blue because Mother nearly died and the hospital called a "code blue."

Things weren't working out too well in Arizona, so Daddy decided we should move back to Arkansas. At least Grandma Betsy would get better now, since she had been to a healing service and the great evangelist, Reverend A. A. Allen, had laid his hands on her.

When we got back to Arkansas, Grandma Betsy and her husband, Donny, a short little man with round cheeks and roving eyes, got an apartment in one of the projects in North Little Rock. I didn't meet Grandma's first husband, my daddy's dad, until I was twelve or so, but when I did, I decided that Grandma positively traded down when she gave him up for Grandpa Donny. And that was before I heard about the shooting match.

You see, Grandpa Arnold, Grandma's first husband, married her when she was only sixteen and showed up pregnant with his one and only child. He was a mature man of twenty-five or so, and I heard he had an awful temper. Grandma might have been with child, but she wasn't ready to settle down yet—and she proved it by bringing her men friends by the house for supper when Grandpa Arnold was off cutting timber.

Grandpa, they say, thought Grandma Betsy was the prettiest little thing he'd ever seen and he'd go an buy her a whole wardrobe of beautiful clothes when he got his logging check. Then he'd get home and run into one of her men friends and he'd take the whole bunch of just-bought pretty dresses out back and burn 'em. It seemed like a pure waste of money to me, but I guess I can understand.

Anyway, after the baby was born, Grandma Betsy's mother and Gibb, her step-dad, fell in love with their firstborn grandchild and decided Grandpa Arnold should just stay away and not bother them anymore.

Grandpa Arnold didn't like the sound of that, so he came around whenever he wanted to see his baby boy. One day he came to call and Gibb got out his shotgun and chased Grandpa

Arnold off his land. The next day, Grandpa came back around and caught Gibb out in the field. He got his attention by firing off a shot and kept shooting after Gibb took to running. As I heard the story told, every time Gibb jumped over a dirt clod or stump, Grandpa Arnold would blast the thing to bits with another round from his shotgun.

That made ol' Gibb pretty mad, so he went into town and reported what Grandpa had done, said the man was trying to kill him.

The Sheriff called up Grandpa Arnold and said, "What you trying to do here, kill ol' Gibb?" I heard there wasn't much love lost between Gibb and the town law officers because Gibb was always getting in trouble when he got drunk.

"I wasn't trying to kill him," Grandpa Arnold said, his blue eyes sparkling like the clear water of the White River flowing by just a few feet away. "If I'd been trying to kill him, he'd be dead."

Well, Grandpa Arnold had to prove his claim. They say the sheriff took a quarter and stuck it in an oak tree all the way across the White River. Then he challenged Grandpa Arnold to shoot it out of there. If he could hit the quarter, then wasn't trying to kill Gibb. If he missed, he was going to jail for attempted murder.

The whole town got excited about the quarter-shoot and came out to line the banks of the White River to see if Grandpa Arnold could shoot the quarter out of that tree.

Grandpa took his time lining that quarter up in his sights, and pulled the trigger. Sure enough, the bullet from Grandpa's shotgun hit the quarter and drove it deep into the bark of that old oak tree.

They say Grandpa didn't come around much after that, but he never had another woman as far as anyone knew and he never got married again. He moved on up the White River valley and lived the life of a hermit until he died.

Not long after that, a young man named Donny came along and asked Grandma's hand in marriage. Most folks said he was a steady worker and would likely make a good father to her boy, so Grandma Betsy married him. She never let him adopt her boy, and I always wondered if Grandma still had a tender place in her heart for her childhood sweetheart.

Grandpa Donny did the best he could, but having very little education and not a lot of personality, he had to settle for menial jobs that didn't pay a lot. That's why he and Grandma were glad to get an apartment in the North Little Rock Housing Authority Projects.

I wasn't sure why they called it a project, but I thought it had something to do with being poor, because most people who lived there didn't own a car and those who did weren't bragging about it. There was a bunch of squirts from the great big gun in the sky after that since I got to spend lots of days at Grandma's house and she stood me on a stool and let me help her bake. She even put an apron on me and tied it around my waist. I knew, if anybody loved me, Grandma did.

That's why I was really disappointed when Grandma started getting sick again. I heard the Reverend A.A. Allan was arrested for drunk driving. I don't know if Grandma lost her faith after hearing that, or if God changed his mind about all those healings He'd handed out when the Rev. Allen laid his hands on folks, but I do know Grandma's sickness came back. She couldn't stand up for long periods of time and she got really sad. I didn't get to go over there much after that, just an occasional visit or to spend the night.

I don't think anyone, anywhere, could have had a better time at Christmas than us Davenports did~

Chapter 4

One of the reasons we left Arizona and came back to Arkansas had to do with a Christmas tree—at least that's what my daddy said.

Christmas was always a happy time in the Davenport house. There were lots of secrets—good secrets—that time of the year. Mother and Daddy whispered together right in front of our faces, hinting at Christmas morning surprises. They always went shopping together on Christmas Eve to take advantage of last minute sales. We always had a real live tree with bunches of presents wrapped and laid out under it.

O'dell, our blue baby, was born in Arizona on November 22, and after all the sadness and near tragedy, Daddy set out to spend the few dollars he had in his pocket on a Christmas tree. That's when he discovered people of limited means might as well not try to put up a big green pine tree or blue spruce. They just weren't to be had. He settled instead for a wimpy little plant that came about waist high—and the thing died before

Christmas. After that, Daddy decided to move the Davenport family back to Arkansas.

The next year we had our usual feast with a golden brown turkey, homemade corn bread, and a big ol' evergreen tree. Mother put out little bowls of nuts and hard candy and there were all the apples and oranges we could eat.

We were not allowed, under any circumstances, to pass through the hallway on Christmas morning to get into all those treasures sitting under that tree until Daddy had had his breakfast. Mother made him eggs and bacon and all of us kids sat on his bed or on mother's bed and watched him eat it. When he was done, he got the camera and went ahead of us into the living room while we lined up, youngest to oldest, and got ready to run for it as soon as he said, *Go!*

I don't know what happened to all those Christmas pictures, but I loved them because Christmas was one of the few times we captured everyone smiling on camera at the same time.

One of my favorites caught everyone in motion. It must have been taken a few years after our journey to Arizona, because O'dell looked to be about seven. The only person missing was Willy, because he wasn't born yet, and Dustin—but I'll get to that later.

In the photograph, O'dell was running around, riding a stick horse. A floppy cowboy hat seemed glued to his head, making him look even taller and skinnier. You'd never know that just a few weeks ago our camera-happy daddy held O'dell by his ankles over a torrent of muddy water on its way to the sea, trying, in Daddy's words, "to teach him a lesson."

Mitch was tearing into something mechanical and Dora, beautiful golden-haired Dora, was lost in a wonderland of flying mane and squeaky springs atop a plastic stallion anchored to four metal posts. She happily rocked back and forth, waving her hands in the air like Annie Oakley.

I'm not sure what Suzanne was doing, but whatever it was I know she was doing it with straight-backed dignity, because that's the only way I ever saw Suzanne do anything—tall, and straight, and elegant.

When we got older, we started taking trips at Christmas to see "the relatives," but we'll get to that later. I don't think anyone, anywhere, could have had a better time at Christmas than us Davenports did, and I think we were all glad to be back home in Arkansas where we belonged.

"Spare the rod," he said, "and spoil the child." The words came right out of the good book so I never questioned it.

Chapter 5

It was 1957 and Dustin was six years old. Everybody loved my brother. He was the model child, not like me. I talked too much. Dustin was quiet and pensive with a big-toothed smile that reached from one side of his face clear to the other. A few freckles, the same color as his eyes, dusted his nose. Dustin took care of me like a big brother is supposed to—he always had my back. I don't think he knew he was the favored one. He just lived his life and tried to be good.

One day we were playing together when Dustin said something that made me mad. I think it must have been my crazy red hair that stirred my temper, for everybody knew Dustin never did anything wrong. Fool that I was, I stuck my tongue out at him. He promptly spit on it. Without a second's hesitation, I slapped his face. I held my breath and felt my heart stand still. What had I done? I had slapped the firstborn son.

Instantly, Daddy was at my side. He grabbed my arm, startling me. "Why'd you do that?" Without giving me time to answer, he demanded, "Apologize to your brother."

Words forsook me. Anyone who knows me now may think I am lying, because I am never at a loss for words. But so many words, and so much fear of saying them, melded together like cold oatmeal and clumped together in my throat. I shook my head.

"I told you to apologize to your brother!"

I couldn't believe what I did next. Out of all the words rolling around in my head, the only one that came out was "no." I don't think my daddy knew what to do with that. None of us kids ever said no to him. I don't know which we feared the most, his belt or hell fire, but we were sure kids who refused to obey their parents deserved both.

I don't know what got into me, but whatever it was held on to my heart like a pit bull dog. The more that Daddy insisted I apologize, the more vehemently I shook my head. The next thing I knew the belt was coming out. That dreaded one-inch width of leather could sting like a wasp and leave angry welts on our legs and butt long after he'd threaded it back into his pants.

Mother stood over in the corner looking miserable. I knew I'd get no help from her. Daddy's word was law in our house, and his belt was the instrument of torture by which we paid for our crimes. When he was done with us, Mother was allowed to follow up by applying alcohol to our wounds. She didn't seem to take any pleasure in it. Sometimes, I think she might have been crying—you know, that silent kind of crying that shows up in your eyes and turns your face red but no tears come out. Since Daddy didn't want her comforting us after he did his work on us, I thought doctoring us might be Mother's way of trying to make us feel better. Daddy allowed it because there was no need to risk infection and give someone the idea that he might have done something wrong. He just did what every good daddy did—he corrected his children. "Spare the rod," he often said, "and spoil the child." The words came right out of the Good Book, so I never questioned it.

• • •

The saddest part about the whole thing was Dustin's remorse. He would have gladly stuck out his tongue and let me bathe it in spit before he would have seen me take a beating. Heck, he usually lied and said he did it, whatever the wrong was, before he'd let me take a beating.

Dustin knew me better than anyone else. He didn't know about our cultural heritage or he might have understood my Irish temper and my Dutch obstinacy. All he knew was that my sense of justice was refined beyond my years and I would likely die before I would apologize to him after suffering the indignity of his spit on my tongue.

His sadness grew during the years to come, finally boiling over when he was nine years old. I would have gladly apologized to him then if it would have made a difference, but of course, by then it was too late.

The one I was concerned about at five years of age wasn't Dustin and it wasn't me. It was Daddy. I had never seen him so mad. The belt rose and fell over and over, and I screamed and cried, but I did not, I could not, bring myself to give him the one word he wanted. I wasn't sorry and I couldn't say I was.

There are some moments in our lives that stick in our mind like the point of a compass. They change the direction of our living and sometimes even our dying. That moment came for me when my daddy gave up on me. He picked me up and threw me across the bed where I landed in a crumpled pile. He turned on his heel, dropping his belt on the bed as if it had failed him, and muttered two words that would change my life, "Damn you."

Daddy never swore, and he taught us that those who do are in danger of hell fire. I had done this. My stubbornness had driven him to swear. Worse than that, he had turned his back on me. I was sure he would never come back. Who would play games with me and tuck me into bed? No one else knew how to play "skin the rabbit." And what if he went to hell and it was my fault? I knew hell was a horrible place. People burn up forever down there and are thirsty all the time. They are always alone and no one ever helps them. I thought I might know a little about what hell felt like, but I didn't. Not then.

Imagine my joy when Daddy came back. A few hours after stomping out the door, he returned and I ran to him. I don't remember running into his arms, but I remember my relief that he didn't hate me. Later he was to say, "I thought Chelsey had won when she held out against me and wouldn't apologize when I wore my belt out on her. But after that, she always did as I said. Everything was, 'yes sir.'"

He was right. I had tasted the bitter waters of emotional abandonment and had my fill. I would die before I would go through that again. In a way, perhaps I did die, but my body kept on breathing, and talking, and walking, except now it felt more like an extension of my daddy than a real part of me.

What I wanted, needed, or believed didn't matter. What mattered was not being alone in a cold cruel world.

Vague pieces of memories float back and forth through my mind but can't seem to connect at the right places to provide a complete picture~

Chapter 6

I understood at an early age that we were better off than most of my relatives. My parents were not about to accept a handout from the government. I wished they would. My mother's grandmother, Grandma Abby, was elderly and got food from the state department of welfare. Her refrigerator was never without a block of cheese as long as my arm and fresh milk made up from powder that came in a cardboard box. I was glad when we went to stay with her for awhile. She had a spare room in her little corner grocery store behind her own apartment, and she offered it to my parents until we got settled. That is why I was sleeping in the bed between my daddy and mother. I think I liked it.

I don't remember ever being held and rocked, or cuddled, but I know daddy sometimes got me dressed for bed. That's when we played, "skin the rabbit." He stripped my dirty clothes away with a flourish and got me into my pajamas. I remember giggling, enjoying the attention. All that changed one night as

I shared a bed with him and my very pregnant mother. Vague pieces of memory float back and forth through my mind, but can't seem to connect at the right places to provide a complete picture. I woke up early the next morning and realized my panties were on the floor beside the bed. I crawled out and put them on, a sickness rising inside me that threatened to close up my throat.

Perhaps that is why I got into so much trouble after I was shipped off to Newport to stay with Aunt Judith, my daddy's aunt, until the baby was born. I don't think the visit lasted for more than a week, but what happened before, and the things that happened when I got there, just about convinced me that there weren't any more squirts left in the gun.

• • •

I was sad to leave home, but excited when my Newport cousins told me I would actually get to work in the cotton fields. I would have my own little sack and work right along with them every day of my vacation. Two of the cousins were twins and I thought they were really pretty. They took me to school with them one day and I was wowed by their popularity. Everybody liked them, especially the boys.

So when they came to my bed a few nights after I arrived and told me they had a secret, I felt privileged. Finally, I had someone who wanted to play with me. They were glad I came! At first, I liked what they did. It felt good. And it made me feel like I was really a part of their peer group. After all, they wouldn't do this to just anybody. And then, they left me and went to their own beds. The darkness closed in over me and I recognized a familiar slimy feeling somewhere deep inside. I was a bad girl. I already knew that. The sick feeling I had felt when I found my panties on the floor in my Great-Grandmother's extra bedroom returned and I just wanted to go home.

To make matters worse, I got sun poisoning. I didn't know what it was then, and the twins and their friends ridiculed me for it. "You're just a city sissy," they said, "can't even last a day in the cotton field." I never considered that my red hair and pale complexion may have contributed to my misery—I just knew I was throwing up my guts and no one seemed to care. No one except Buddy.

Buddy cared. He was the twin's older brother, much older. I heard later that Buddy had killed someone and spent years in prison for it. He didn't seem like a murderer. He looked at me with tender eyes like the dear old hound dog that lazed away the hot summer days on the wooden porch. He never said anything, but when I got sick, he brought me an Almond Joy candy bar. It was my favorite. I wondered how he knew—or was it just coincidence that he picked the very candy I loved best? I even dared to wonder, just a little bit, if someone or something might have whispered "Almond Joy" in his ear when he thought of me at the store. It was enough that he thought of me at all. If he had brought me a chocolate-covered pickle, I think I would have eaten it out of pure gratitude.

Every day I begged to go home and every day I was told, "Not until the baby comes." I prayed for the baby to come quickly. I'm sure my mother's labor pains were a direct answer to my prayers, for within a week, on exactly June 18th, my very own birthday, my sister Suzanne came into the world. They didn't have a crib for her so they brought her home and put blankets in the bottom of a pulled-out drawer. It would do for a while.

When they brought me home, they told me I had a birthday present waiting. When I saw the tiny baby laying there in that wooden drawer just like a porcelain doll, waving her fists at me, I was hooked. I would have done anything for her. She was mine. *My very own birthday present.* She even had red hair, just like me. I don't remember much about Suzanne after that—not until I was a teenager and she was a skinny, freckled-face little girl who insisted on keeping the drapes closed because she'd heard that even the teeniest drop of sunlight makes freckles grow bigger. Didn't she know that her hazel eyes and perfect oval face made a proper setting for those dime sized freckles? Why, even the copper red hair that flowed down Suzanne's ram-rod straight back accented the picture of a blossoming beauty, if one stopped long enough to take note of it.

You'd think, with me being newly-turned six years old and coming home to my own living-doll baby sister, I'd remember holding her, rocking her, and maybe even burping her a time or two. But if I have any memories of Baby Suzanne, they have gone off somewhere to hide—maybe someday they'll come back to me and I'll take them out, like the 1957 Christmas picture, and get to know the baby sister I had but don't remember.

I was so glad to be home that the memory of the danger lurking in the privacy of my parent's borrowed bedroom managed to hide itself beneath the clutter of all that had happened over the past week. I had learned that the feeling of stinky green slime sliding across something inside me was more common than I had supposed.

Chapter 7

Looking into the past is a lot like staring into a deep well. I know there's water down there, because I can hear it splash if I throw a rock into it. I know, too, that all kinds of dangerous things live down there—things that would bite and sting and maybe even kill me if I dared go down into it. I guess the only thing that drives a sane person to lower herself into it is getting real thirsty. If I want water badly enough, I might risk the danger to get to the bottom of the well.

Sometimes, the water comes to you. Maybe the water condenses and settles on a cloud and then when the cloud gets heavy enough, it falls out of the sky and onto your head. That's what happened to me one day when I was seven or eight years old.

A little girl down the street named Debra wanted to be my friend. I knew friendship could be risky, because I was already sure that there were some major differences in me and everyone else and it would bring that slimy feeling right to the surface if anyone should discover what they were. But what little girl can resist friends forever? So, I started walking the two or three blocks down the street—which seemed like a long way to me at the time—to play with her.

The sun was shining like it was smiling down on me. I had a friend and she wanted to play with me. We made a picnic lunch of bread cut into tiny pieces, a few slices of an apple, and a handful of raisins. Finding a twisted oak that looked like it might house the jolly green giant in its top branches, we spread a blanket on the ground and sat down for our feast. Debra was one of those baby-doll girls who liked to play Mama. That didn't bother me too much until she looked me square in the face and said, "I'll be the Mama and you can be the Dad."

I don't know what came over me. Maybe the sky opened up and dropped one of those big ol' raindrops I was talking about, because suddenly I was soaked. I broke out in sweat and when I opened my mouth to tell her I didn't want to be a dad, that I never wanted to be a dad, the words got stuck in my throat. I jumped up and ran all the way home. Debra never came over again and I avoided her house like the plague. Every time I went past it, I looked the other way, but it still made me feel slimy in that secret place.

• • •

Most of the time, my only playmates were my siblings—especially Dustin. Whatever Dustin said, that was my rule. Like the time he made me stop hanging upside down on the monkey bars at school.

What happened was that I had gotten some new panties. Not just any old panties. These were amazing panties, the kind a rich girl might wear. They were white with tiny red ruffles sown right across the butt. I had already put them on in front of the mirror and admired how they covered me just right. None of my private parts showed, but the way a ruffle wrapped itself around the elastic at the leg opening was terribly flattering.

Now how is a girl to show off something as elegant as a fancy pair of underwear? The monkey bars at school were just the right thing. I could hang upside down, allowing my dress to billow over my face and swing back and forth so that everyone would see that I had something to show off. I imagined every girl in the schoolyard envying me and all the boys thinking a princess had come among them and they didn't even know it until that moment.

It's a good thing that my dress covered my face so I couldn't see the way my behavior affected my classmates, because I heard about it later and my white skin blushed all shades of red.

I went through the rest of the school day enjoying the side glances of my peers. They didn't know I could be so pretty, I told myself, already plotting how I could get mother to buy me another pair of ruffled panties, this time with blue ruffles, or maybe green.

I was still on cloud nine when the bell rang and Dustin met me as he always did at the front door. I came to the door smiling, my good news ready to bubble over all the way home. That's when I noticed Dustin was angry. Not just a little bit, he was mad. And he had a shiner under his eye. My bubbles all burst when I realized he had been in a fight.

Something heavy squeezed the blood out of my heart and I knew, I just knew, something dreadful had happened and it was my fault. Dustin wouldn't take my hand like he always did, but walked along beside me in silence. Finally I got up the nerve to ask, "What happened?"

"Got in a fight."

"You never fight."

It was true. Dustin was one of the few boys in the schoolyard who never got in fist fights. One reason is that everyone loved him—except the bullies. They didn't love anybody. They just loved to pick on younger kids and there was a bunch of them in our neighborhood.

I would never forget the time the bullies locked Mitch—my two-years-younger brother—and O'dell—the "blue baby"—in an old shed and we didn't find them until late that night when our search took us near the shed and we heard them yelling for help. The bullies took after Dustin and me every once in a while, and most times we managed to outrun them.

Once, Dustin scared me to death by grabbing my hand and dragging me into a storm drain when he saw them coming. He was afraid of them, but I would have rather faced those boys than the dark and the snakes and spiders that inhabited it.

Finally, Dustin looked me full in the face and said, "Don't ever hang upside down on the monkey bars like that again." I nodded full of knowing and hating it. I never asked for the new panties with the blue ruffles.

Chapter 8

Somehow Daddy's mama and step-dad ended up moving in with us. I don't know why it happened, maybe because Grandma Betsy got sick so much, but I was glad it did.

My grandma and step-grandpa didn't really seem to fit together. Grandma was at least five-foot-nine and couldn't have weighed an ounce over a hundred pounds. What she lacked in physical strength, she made up for with a bold, brave spirit. Grandpa Donny was short, stout, and mostly silent. Mother said he had eyes for other women . . . whatever that meant.

I thought Grandma loved Dustin better than me, but I could understand that. I was a really bad girl and Dustin was good. It was only right. But she loved me, too. I knew she did and that made me almost happy.

She must have been in the hospital sometimes, because I don't remember her being around very much. But Grandpa Donny was, and he started showing me a lot of affection. I ate it up like cream-cheese icing on carrot cake.

One day I was sitting in his lap watching something on TV and feeling especially affectionate. I remember he was holding me real tight and I reached up and kissed his cheek. I felt his arms tighten around me and that was when I knew Grandpa loved me.

Just then, Mother charged over and pulled me off his lap. I was startled, and couldn't understand the angry look on her face. She rarely seemed to notice me and I wondered what I could have done wrong. She bent over me and held on to both my arms, giving me a little shake. "Don't you ever let him touch you like that again." She ordered.

I nodded but said nothing. I didn't know what to say. I didn't know what "like that" meant. Hadn't he just held me on his lap, like everyone else held Dustin, and hadn't he just given me a hug? Wasn't I supposed to love my grandpa and wasn't it okay for him to love me back?

Then I got it. That slimy feeling crept back up, all the way to my throat. I went out the back door and walked around awhile, trying to figure out how I could turn myself into someone else, someone who didn't always mess everything up. Finally, I came to the realization that it wasn't so much what I did as who I was. I was the second-born child, a girl with wild red hair and no redeeming qualities. How could I expect to be held and loved or treated like anyone special?

I knew I was on the right track with this a few days later. I had gone to bed early, maybe for a nap. Apparently night had fallen while I slept because when I opened my eyes it was pitch black. At first I thought I was alone, then I noticed a reddish glow near the door that opened into the hallway. As I stared at it, I realized that I was staring into the eyes of a black dog. He was the size of a poodle, but his hair was ebony and as wiry as a stiff hairbrush. His ears stuck straight up and his red eyes glared at me as if he wanted to leap on me and tear me apart. I didn't move and neither did he. I was aware of voices coming from the living room just around the corner. Mother, Daddy and Grandpa were watching something on TV and laughing their heads off. Didn't they know I was facing death in the next room?

I tried to call for help, but no sound came out. I took the only reasonable course of action. I slid down under the blankets and covered my head. Eventually I must have fallen asleep, because I woke the next morning and the dog was gone. That's when I realized my family didn't know. They didn't know anything. They couldn't see the dog and they couldn't see me. Both of us were pretty much invisible and neither of us were reason enough to interrupt a perfectly good TV show.

Soon after that, my grandparents moved out and we moved into a different house in a nearby neighborhood. I went into a different school—much to my relief. We could finally forget about the incident on the monkey bars. I think that's when I learned moving wasn't so bad after all.

If a merry heart does good like a medicine, we overdosed right out there in our own backyard~

Chapter 9

We changed schools, but not much else. At least I had Dustin to play with and walk me down to Great-grandma Abby's store, which was only a few blocks away. I don't remember much about the other kids during this time. I wonder if they weren't in the bottom of the well somewhere, swimming around, doing their thing while I remained topside doing mine. I do remember one thing, of which I am very much ashamed.

Dustin and I played a trick on our six-year-old brother Mitch that got us both into trouble, but at the time we thought it was worth it. Dustin initiated the trick, but who would believe that? He came to me, holding a bright red hot pepper in his hand. He said, "I am so sick of him (Mitch) tattling on us and getting us into trouble. I'm gonna teach him a lesson." That sounded good to me. This is how it happened.

Dustin hid the red pepper in his hand, allowing just the tip of it to show. He offered me a bite right in front of Mitch. Being two years younger than me, Mitch fell right into it. "What you got?" he asked.

"Oh, nothin'," Dustin said, pretending to nibble on the pepper and licking his lips. He held his hands out to me and I added the appropriate sound effects, "Umm," and smacking my lips.

"I want some!" Mitch wailed.

We let him carry on for a while before Dustin finally relented and said, "Okay, but just a taste, okay?" He opened his hands and Mitch grabbed the pepper and stuffed the whole thing into his mouth. It took all of three seconds before the pain hit him. If you've ever eaten a red pepper, the kind that looks all shiny and waxy from drying out in the sun, then you know it feels like a whole nest of hornets are trapped in your mouth.

Mitch opened his mouth wide and started gulping in deep breaths. Then he took off for the house, screaming like his pants were on fire. Mother met him at the door and I was pleased to see that her murderous look included Dustin this time and not just me. Both of us ran for our lives. We doubled over behind the green branched forsythia bushes and laughed until we cried. Every time we looked at each other, waves of delicious laughter rolled over us and we were as helpless as a cricket in a riptide to hold it in. Our breath came in ragged snatches and our faces were purple with oxygen deprivation. If a merry heart doeth good like a medicine as the Good Book says, we overdosed right out there in our own backyard.

After awhile we got hungry and went in for supper. The mosquitoes had taken ample bites out of us, but that didn't keep us from grinning from ear to ear. Apparently, mother had relinquished her anger at us by suppertime and we got off without so much as a whipping over the whole deal. Mitch wouldn't look at either of us, but after a day or two I think he dumped the whole thing into his own personal well and went on as if nothing had happened.

You'd think that since my siblings were mostly my only playmates, I'd have a lot of memories of growing up with them, but those memories, if I have any, must be mixed up with some others that found their way into the well, because I can't bring much up.

It seems to me that I lived a lot of my childhood in my dreams, if indeed that's what they were. One dream that I had when I was in the second grade came at me over and over. Does that mean it was trying to tell me something? Maybe it would have if I could have figured it out back then, or told someone about it other than my mother.

• • •

In the dream, I am in our backyard, which has an old fence around it with a wooden gate. There I am, all of eight years old, standing at the gate, when three mafia-looking men come up in our yard. The sun glints off their spit-shined shoes and I think they might be handsome if they weren't out to get me. They don't look mean, but I know why they've come.

They head right for me, moving fast. Panic seizes me and I lock my fingers down hard on the wooden fence. I turn my head in every direction, but there is no one around to help me.

I don't know where the other kids are, but I can see my mother. She is in the house standing at the kitchen sink . . . I think she's singing. I try to call out to her, but not a sound squeezes through my throat. I want to run, but I can't move.

They come right up to the fence and start prying my fingers off the gate. Their car is at the curb, doors open, motor running. I can feel my hold on the gate slipping, and I try to scream, but I can't get out a sound. They're getting me, here I go, and mother keeps singing. There is a beautiful smile on her face as she looks right past me at the tree line and lets me go.

• • •

Sometimes, after this dream, I'd wake up screaming and mother would come to my bed. She'd bring me water and try to comfort me. I'm actually kind of glad about the dreams, because that is the only memory I have of mother from my early years except when she doctored my welts with alcohol after Daddy whipped me, and I didn't like her then because she watched him do it. At least, she couldn't see the men in my dreams so she didn't know what was happening. If she knew, she would have stopped it. I was sure of it.

I don't know if it was the dreams or something else that was happening that I don't remember, but something took my appetite away at eight years old. I started losing weight.

"Chelsey, you've got to eat," Mother said. She finally went to Dr. White, our family physician, and told him she couldn't get me to eat. He told her to put me on half-and-half milk and see if that fixed it. I tried to drink the thick milk, but couldn't get it down. Finally, Dr. White put me in the hospital.

It's strange how I don't remember Daddy during any of this time. He was usually the one to take care of me. I loved it that Mother came to see me in the hospital and for some reason, I was glad Daddy didn't come. I knew I was crazy then, because I wanted him to come and I didn't. It was almost like I wanted a part of him to come, but I couldn't get that part without the rest so I decided I was glad he just stayed home.

They kept me in the hospital two weeks and gave me ice cream. The nurses were nice and said sweet things about my eyes. They patted my arm when they came in and smiled a lot. I wasn't in a hurry to go home, and I started thinking maybe I wasn't such a bad girl after all. If I was really bad, would they smile at me like that and make such a fuss over me? It never occurred to me that they were just doing their job. Even now, I like to think it was more than that. I like to think they really cared about the eight-year-old girl who mysteriously stopped eating and lost a lot of weight.

Thinking about it later, a lot later, I figured out that the stay in Dr. White's hospital saved my life, for it was then that I decided to live. Dustin had a different experience. Maybe if he too had stopped eating and had the chance to take a vacation in the hospital things would have been different. Or maybe they wouldn't have. I guess I'll never know, but I know that what happened next had something to do with Dustin's decision. I know when Dustin decided to die.

There is nothing more romantic than the long drawn whistle of the midnight train~

Chapter 10

On second thought, maybe Dustin didn't exactly decide to die when I was eight and he was nine, maybe he just quit caring about living and the forces of nature took care of the rest.

We had moved again. Daddy bought a house from a church and had it moved to a vacant lot. Mother painted the living room sea-foam green. She hung a picture of a ship in a storm over the couch. I used to get lost in that picture, wishing I could go to sea.

We lived near a railroad track and I'd lie awake at night and listen for the lonely whistle of the midnight train. I'd imagine the conductor tugging at the rope to make it blow and almost convince myself he was telling me good-bye as he rumbled through on his way to other lands. There is nothing more romantic than the long, drawn whistle of the midnight train.

• • •

About that time, Daddy, who had always been a car mechanic, decided he wanted to go into real estate. Mother would do it with him and they would be a real go-getter real estate team. They started working on passing their real estate test. Mother was smarter than Daddy, and found it to be a breeze, which didn't set too well with him. They started arguing a lot, but kept studying and working on it. It seems to me I was in the second grade about this time, but it's really hard to hang your life on a timeline when you've measured it mostly by the recollection of events you'd just as soon forget.

I guess we still owned the shotgun house we'd lived in across from the cotton patch in Newport, because Daddy started making trips to Newport to fix it up. He'd see our relatives when he went there—Aunt Molly who was Grandma Betsy's sister, and her husband, Uncle Harry. He'd sometimes visit Aunt Judith, who I was fond of even if I did get sick at her house and want to go home. So when he told Dustin and me that we could go to Newport with him, we were both excited. My excitement was tinged with something else that I couldn't explain. It was like the critters at the bottom of my well were making some waves and I felt it in the pit of my stomach. I pushed that out of my mind and looked forward to getting a break from the monotonous everyday life I lived at home. I have learned to pay attention when my stomach gets that certain feeling, but I hadn't learned that yet.

Dustin and I were tired after the two-hour drive, and a little bored. We walked around the house and investigated everything that got our interest, but that wasn't much. And then something else happened. I'm not sure what it was, because I can't get down deep enough to figure it out. But I know it was bad. I know it is what brought Dustin to his decision. Back then I just knew that something had plunged itself into my heart and it was twisting every which way. Somehow, I knew something worse was going to happen, and I couldn't do anything about it. Something terrible was going to happen, and it was my fault.

It happened when we got to Aunt Molly's house. We were going to spend the night there and go home in the morning. Aunt Molly made us a regular country feast like she always did. I loved her house, though most people would say it was more of a shack. It stood on concrete block piers that allowed the chickens to take to the shade underneath. It had four rooms and an outhouse. I never went to the outhouse. I knew the company those places kept—rattlesnakes and copperheads, black widow spiders and yucky bugs and worms. I wanted nothing to do with the outhouse, so I made sure I didn't drink anything near bedtime and didn't eat very much at Aunt Molly's and Uncle Harry's house.

It was worth putting up with the outhouse to visit Aunt Molly. Some people aren't meant to be movie stars, and Aunt Molly was one of them, but she was a star to me. Everything she did, from her southern drawl to her home cooking was as natural as could be. I loved watching her dip her snuff. She didn't just dip it—she made a ceremony out of it. She carried a covered fruit jar around with her and just before the brown juice began to trickle down the corners of her mouth, she'd unscrew and remove the lid, take careful aim and squirt the shiny stream into the fruit jar. She'd reattach the lid and set the jar down nearby, always within close reach. From the satisfaction on her face, I'd say her simple ritual contributed immensely to Aunt Molly's daily joy.

Uncle Harry was tall and angular with a strong jaw. He never said much, but I liked him. He seemed righteous somehow—you know, like he'd never do anything wrong. I'd heard that he and Aunt Molly had suffered a family tragedy. Their first child (and they only had one other) was born with a third eye right in the middle of her forehead. She only lived a few weeks but left her mark on Uncle Harry and Aunt Molly for a lifetime. I couldn't look at them without thinking about that poor three-eyed baby and feeling sorry for them. Every time I thought about the baby who died I wanted to cry. I think maybe I did cry, a little.

Maybe that's why I didn't cry when Daddy did what he did to Dustin. Or maybe beatings were just something I had gotten used to. He didn't beat me much anymore—mostly just the boys—but Dustin didn't get a lot of it. I figured it was because he was so good, but also because he was the firstborn son. Gosh, he was even named after Daddy. Daddy was Dusty and my brother was Dustin. Beating Dustin would be almost like beating yourself, wouldn't it? Of course, I realized later that Daddy used all his names up on the boys. Daddy's name was Dusty Mitchell O'dell, and he named his boys Dustin, Mitchell, and O'dell. He ran out of names by the last one, so he named him after mother's Dad. That was before he had a falling out with Grandpa, and by then he couldn't take it back, so William Bereford Davenport stuck on my youngest brother.

Maybe Daddy thought that he could make the boys turn out like himself if he gave each of them his name, but if he did he was mistaken. They all grew up and none of them turned out a bit like him.

I didn't see Daddy beat Dustin at Aunt Molly's house. I was there. I was right there, but somehow I don't remember any of it. I heard about it later, but somehow my brain was all confused. I remember the chickens going under the house and

I remember the sun shimmering on the little dust bunnies that swirled off the road like miniature tornados. I remember fixing my eyes on the big twisted oak tree that occupied the center of the field and wondering why the farmers left it there when it meant they would have to drive their tractors around it every time they planted and harvested their soy beans or whatever else they planted in the field. I even remember the smell of chicken squat and the fragrance of Aunt Molly's snuff, but I don't remember the beating that changed my life and Dustin's forever.

If the layers of guilt kept piling up in my heart, it was bound to shut down from all that excess weight~

Chapter 11

I heard about it when I got home. I heard Mother and Daddy arguing about it. Aunt Molly had called mother and told her the whole story. She was Daddy's aunt, but she was a kind woman and wouldn't let her kinship get in the way of helping her great-nephew. I wondered why I didn't know what happened to Dustin when I was right there, but I didn't wonder too hard, for I might figure it out and I think I knew I would have changed my mind about the decision I made at Dr. White's hospital. Dustin and I would have gotten together and figured out some way of doing what we needed to do together, but I don't think he would have wanted that. In fact, I know he didn't and that's why we didn't talk to each other after we got home from Newport. We didn't talk to each other at all, except one time.

Daddy seemed to be in a bad mood all the time. He was putting in a new sidewalk up to our front door and he gave me the job of pulling all the grass out between the rocks before the truck came and filled up the forms with concrete. I pulled at it and hated the heat of the sun on my head. I hated everything and I didn't want to do what Daddy said. So I did it half-heartedly, pulling a patch of grass here and there and leaving the rest. I knew that would get me a beating, but at the time I just didn't care.

Dustin came out to take a look. "You know you'll get a beating if you leave all that grass in there," he said without looking at me. Dustin never looked at me anymore.

I shrugged. Who cares.

Then Daddy came out of the house and I saw his lips thin out and turn white. His eyes narrowed into ice blue slits. "I thought I told you to get the grass out of there. What have you been doing?"

"Oh, we traded jobs," Dustin lied. I shouldn't have been surprised. It wasn't the first time he took a beating for me, but for some reason it hurt worse this time. I knew I should have stood up and told Daddy the truth, but old habits are hard to break. Besides, it was too late. If I told now, I would get it for dilly-dallying and Dustin would get it for lying. If the layers of guilt kept piling up in my heart, it was bound to shut down soon from all that excess weight.

• • •

Mother and Daddy kept arguing. Then Mother got the flu. It was bad. I remembered Aunt Molly saying Dustin went out into the backyard and threw up after Dad beat him so badly at her house. I wondered if Mother really had the flu or if she was just so miserable that she threw up like Dustin did.

It was about two weeks after we got back from Newport when my world crumpled into little pieces and scattered itself to the wind. Mother was in bed and needed liquids. She couldn't keep water down, so she sent Dustin to the store for some Diet Coke™. The store was only a few blocks away and he made the trip so often it didn't seem like a big deal.

Then we heard the sound of tires squealing at the intersection just one half-block from our house. Park Avenue was a busy street and the traffic moved along fast. A neighbor came over to the house and told Mother her boy had been hit by a car. The stone I had been carrying in the pit of my stomach for the past two weeks dropped all the way to my feet. I started to follow Mother as she staggered down the street, and I felt like a zombie moving in slow motion. She motioned me to go back to the house and stay with the kids. The look on her face must have mirrored mine—all scrunched up in fear and pain. We knew, I think we both knew, that tragedy had visited us and nothing would ever be the same.

I don't know how long Dustin was in the hospital, but they wouldn't let me go see him. They said he looked terrible and it would be too hard on me to see him like that. As always, I accepted everything they said and walked around with a fogged-up brain trying to act like a real person, when I knew what I appeared to be and what I was deep down were two entirely different things.

Lots of people cried but nobody cried with me, and that's an entirely different matter~

Chapter 12

Dustin never came home. Sometimes I imagined that he went to the store and just kept on walking and one day he was going to walk back in the door. I had seen my brother head out for the store and I heard the tires squeal. I saw Mother's face all stretched out with grief, but I didn't see the damage the tires did to my brother. Maybe it didn't even happen. Maybe it would be like the car without a driver or the black dog with the glowing red eyes. Surely, I reasoned, if my brother was really at death's door, Daddy and Mother would come home and gather me in their arms and invite me to cry it out on their shoulder. I didn't have much experience in matters of people dying, but I'd watched enough TV to have an opinion about it. My opinions changed after Dustin died, because nothing happened the way I thought it would. Lots of people cried, but no one cried with me, and that's a completely different thing.

That's why I didn't like that series on TV called *The Waltons*. Nothing about it was real. If someone in their family died, I knew there would be a lot of holding and crying on each other's shoulder. There'd be a lot of talking and emotions going on. Some people in the family would get mad and others would get really sad and all of them would use their grief to get close to each other and try to fill up the big hole in their heart by loving each other.

It was Mrs. Donson, the preacher's wife, who came to me and wrapped her coat around me at the funeral. She walked me to the car after my brother was lowered into the ground. I was shaking so badly that my teeth were chattering, but no one else seemed to think it was cold. Mrs. Donson asked if I was all right, and I lied like I always did and said I was fine.

If she had known what had gone on in my mixed-up brain since Dustin went away in the ambulance, she wouldn't have bothered to ask. She would have let me freeze to death or called the cops and told them about it. Then they would have put me in the insane institution where I would have rotted away to this day. I was glad she didn't know.

But I knew. I knew that when they told me Dustin was so banged up he might not come home, I vacillated back and forth between wanting him to come home and wanting him to die. I didn't exactly want him to die, because I couldn't get a grasp on the permanence of death. I just wanted him to stay away. Something had happened that I couldn't remember and that something had come between us like a stone ledge that fell on both our hearts. And I wanted all the relatives who were going to come to Arkansas if Dustin died to come on up to our house and stay. Daddy was really kind to everyone while company was there, especially if his cousin Jamie happened to be one of them. If Dustin died, Aunt Jamie was coming to Arkansas and bringing her three daughters with her. I hoped they would stay for a very long time. Somehow, it seemed like Dustin would want that, too.

But it was different when we went to the gravesite. When I heard the preacher say "dust to dust and ashes to ashes," it hit me like hammer on the head. Dust doesn't come back. It scatters itself to the wind and disappears forever.

What had I done? I had willed my brother into the dust and now he was never coming back. The worst of it was that when they lowered his casket into the ground, they buried his secret with him, but I had to live with mine. I was locked into it. No one knew what happened that day two weeks before—except me, Dustin, and our Daddy. Now it was just Daddy and me, and I couldn't even remember the secret. I just knew that Dustin had made a hole in the screen door of that old rental house and come inside unexpectedly and that it made our Daddy so mad he beat my brother to death. Not on the outside where everyone could see, but he died inside. As soon as he could put his affairs in order, he followed up on the outside.

His affairs were fairly simple. He told his teacher that he wanted to take his work home before the open house, so he could show them to his mother. I know that because his teacher told mother, "It was almost as if Dustin knew he was going to die."

Oh, he knew all right. He had run into the one bully he couldn't protect me from so he did what he had always done. He ran away, except this time he couldn't take me with him. He had to go and I had to stay. Our decisions took us two different ways, ways that diverged into separate woods, and that has made all the difference.

I heard Daddy put his arm around the policeman who killed my brother
and they both cried together~

Chapter 13

Everybody that knew my daddy seemed to think he was a fine, upstanding man. Even when an off-duty police officer ran over his firstborn son, Daddy's tenderhearted generosity came through for everybody to see. He kept talking about that poor man who was rushing home from work, trying to get to his own boy in time to see his ball game, and tears came into Daddy's eyes and flowed down his face, hanging on his chin for a moment before dripping off onto his shirt. He cried even harder when he talked about how that policeman locked himself in his room and wouldn't come out to eat or go to work. When he talked about how that poor man couldn't even stand to look at his own boy because it made him think of Dustin and that was just too hard for him, Daddy knew he had to do something to relieve that poor policeman's suffering.

What he did made him almost revered by everybody who heard about it, and somehow it seemed like everybody in our town had heard.

He went to see that off-duty police officer. He went between the time Dustin died and the day of the funeral. I wasn't there, but I heard that Daddy put an arm around the man who killed my brother and they both cried together. It was enough to soften even the most hardened heart, but it didn't do much for mine. Maybe if Daddy had put his arm around me and cried some tears on my shoulder, I would have cried with him, too. But that didn't happen and we moved on with our lives.

Chapter 14

Every time I heard the wail of an ambulance I forgot everything else I was doing and stared in the direction of the sound. I couldn't think of anything else. It happened often at home since we lived so close to Park Avenue and ambulances came by often. It happened a lot at school, too, because the school was just down the street from my home. I think I hoped someone would notice that the nine-year-old girl who had recently lost her only older brother was really sad. Maybe someone would come over to me and say, "Chelsey, you seem upset. Is it because the siren reminded you of the sound you heard when your brother was run over by a car?" Or maybe someone would just come by and put a hand on my shoulder and squeeze it. Nobody ever did, and I didn't blame them. Maybe they knew what I did—that I had wanted Dustin to die. They wouldn't hate me for it if they knew how badly I wanted him to come back, how much I missed him. It finally clicked in my little brain that people really didn't think about what I did or care about what I wanted. I was invisible.

Now I knew what was wrong with me, what had been wrong all along. I was invisible to everyone except Dustin, and now Dustin was gone. Just because there was no invisible child in the Walton family didn't mean there wasn't one in mine.

• • •

Just before I turned ten, Mother had another baby. That's when Daddy decided to take us to Michigan to work in the blueberry fields for the summer. We would join the migrant workers and work for my mother's uncle. It made me a little sad to see my infant sister turned over to Mother's newly-married sister and left behind. I think I sensed Mother's sadness at leaving her baby, but there was no question about doing it. Daddy said we had to go, and the harvest camp was no proper place for an infant.

We got to Michigan after most other families had arrived, and took the only cabin left. It had one room and was situated near the outhouse. Showers consisted of standing under cold water on a metal platform with a curtain around it for privacy. There was only one shower to accommodate the entire camp, so no one got very many of them. They weren't exactly comfortable anyway.

I learned something new at harvest camp. When everyone has underarm odor, nobody notices anyone else. The heat of the sun during the day predicted the need for showers, but the exhaustion born of twelve hours' hard work guaranteed there would not be a line up for the shower most nights.

• • •

I had more education and culture than any of my migrating cousins, so I found myself unexpectedly popular. That was fun for awhile. Then something happened that busted that bubble just like all the others.

Daddy had hurt his back and took to staying at home in the one-room cabin while Mother and we kids went out to the fields. My cursed red hair and pale complexion once again yielded to sun-sickness. The fact that we lived primarily on blueberries and milk didn't help much either. We may have been too poor to buy groceries, but we were also too proud to ask for help.

To add to my misery, someone reported that I was too slow in the fields. Daddy asked why I couldn't pick berries like my cousins did. He forgot to mention that they had been raised following the harvest camps and had picked blueberries since they were two.

He told me I should be ashamed. I had already noticed that my cousin's rough brown hands flew over the branches, dropping berries into their bucket like raindrops in a hurricane. I cursed my clumsy hands, which were no better at picking berries than cotton bolls. I decided I wasn't good for much.

I threw up most of the night, and the next day Daddy decided I should just stay at the cabin with him to keep out of the heat. I shook my head. "I'm better now. I want to help pick berries." I got out the door before he could argue, jumping up on the flatbed trailer with the migrants just as if I belonged there. When we reached the field, I went behind the outhouse and vomited.

Then came the worst of the worst. My cousin Daisy asked if I could spend the night with her. She had a bigger cabin with two separate rooms. The kids had bunk beds in one of them and their parents' bed was in the living room/kitchen area. I climbed into the top bunk with Daisy, having no idea of the disgrace that was about to befall me. For the first time in my life, I wet the bed.

Daisy, having very little culture and no manners, woke up swearing and yelling, "You peed on me!" I went home with my head hung low. I never told my parents, and don't think Daisy's parents did either, but I had lost my honor among the cousins and spent the rest of the summer alone. My favorite pastime was sitting in front of our cabin with my feet in the fine dust of the road. I piled sun-warmed dust up to my ankles and pretended it was sand.

The imagination is a wonderful thing. It can take us out of the most dreadful circumstances and transform us into something entirely different. I've heard that some people get lost in their imaginary world and forget how to come back. I don't know if that's so bad either.

I read once about a woman whose husband beat her. She couldn't have the children she so desperately craved, and she was fired from her job, which resulted in them becoming homeless and living in a big drainage tunnel under a railroad bridge. When that last thing was taken away, the poor woman just called it quits. She didn't walk in front of a car or anything. She found another way to quit living in a world that treated her so bad. She started living entirely in her imagination. She told everyone she had a new husband and gave birth to a new baby every week. She still didn't have a house to live in, so some kind people came and took her to the hospital up on the hill. I guess she needed lots of care, having so many babies and all.

I had never seen the ocean and never expected to, but I could imagine the dust was sand and the grass was cool blue water. That is when my imagination took wings and began to fly on its own.

Sometimes I guess even presidents get in harms way when people are tired of being bullied~

Chapter 15

We returned to Arkansas in time to start school just after Labor Day. Mrs. Atkins, my fifth grade teacher, was the meanest woman I ever met. She made fun of my unfashionably long dresses, she mimicked me on several occasions, and generally made it known that I was her least favored student. When I didn't listen or talked out of turn, she pulled me up by the ear and gave me a verbal thrashing while my peers scrunched themselves as small as possible in their one-armed chairs.

One day she passed out some books that she said were now out of print and therefore especially precious. After going into detailed instructions about how we were to handle her precious books, Mrs. Atkins asked us to open to the chapter on Theodore Roosevelt, her favorite president. Right in the middle of class I must have done something wrong, because Mrs. Atkins came back to my desk and grabbed my ear. I thought she'd rip it off my head the way she twisted it and yanked it back and forth.

When she was done, she turned on her heel and returned to the front of the class as if nothing had happened.

I looked at her precious book and her favorite president's picture, and knew what I had to do. I am not proud of what I did, but I have to tell you so you'll know how bad I really was. I took the point of my compass, that sharp steel point, and traced around Mr. Roosevelt's picture until it came loose from the page. I lifted it out with two fingers and crumpled it into a tiny wad and put it in my pocket. I knew what I did was wrong, but that didn't keep me from feeling a whole lot better.

The next day Mrs. Atkins came to school and told the class what some awful person had done. She asked for a confession. I looked at her with all the rage a ten-year-old can muster and willed her to know that I was the one who spoiled her prized book. I hoped she'd think about that the next time she tried to pull my ear off.

I wasn't prepared for the look of fear that came into Mrs. Atkins eyes when she looked at me and recognized pure, unadulterated hatred sitting on my face. Mrs. Atkins was a bully who took her petty frustrations out on me, and I was fighting back the only way I knew how. Poor Mr. Roosevelt is the only innocent person in this story because he didn't do anything to have his picture ripped out of a book about presidents. Sometimes I guess even presidents get in harm's way when people are tired of being bullied.

• • •

Daddy finally learned enough to pass his real estate salesman's test. He and mother soon made enough money to buy our first new car—a Ford Fairlane. I thought we were rich. None of our relatives had a new car, or even nearly new. It didn't change our lifestyle much. We still ate bologna sandwiches and milk with cereal from those big plastic bags that are packaged for large families. When I was grown and someone asked me how I wanted my steak, my sincere answer was, "Any way you want to cook it is okay with me."

It wasn't long before Daddy and Mother started arguing again, and this time it was worse. Daddy said Mother took credit for his success in sales, and Mother denied it. Then, Daddy's back got worse. He started staying home more. He had more problems than even I could have imagined.

First of all, he couldn't quit smoking. He was convinced he would go to hell if he didn't give it up, but he just couldn't get it done. It wasn't his fault, really. Most of the time, it was mine. If I had paid more attention, he would have made it through for sure, but I always failed him at just the worst time.

Like the time he had been quit four whole days. He thought the worst was over and I guess I did too, because I went to my room and got my guitar out and started strumming it. I was off in my own little world when he stormed into the room.

"Didn't you hear that phone ring?"

"No, Dad." I put the guitar down on my bed. He kept standing there with his mouth gaping open like somebody who has just told a big lie, so I said, "I didn't hear it."

"Right. You know I can't answer the phone and talk to customers when I am trying to quit smoking. Didn't you even hear it ringing?"

Sometimes I thought Dad had a short attention span, because he often asked the same question twice or even three times.

"No, Dad. I'm really sorry. I didn't hear it."

"I'da had it beat if I could've held out another day. Just one more day."

I hung my head and shut up, knowing I hadn't heard the last of it.

He went outside and smoked some cigarettes while I huddled on my bed. After a while he came back in and every time he passed me, he looked at me with a certain expression that bit into my feelings like a rattlesnake, spreading its poison through me. He looked sad and disappointed, but there was a sting in it too, a blaming look that made sure I didn't forget that I was the one who caused all his hurt.

The other problem my Dad had was an injured back. By the time I turned twelve he was spending most of the day at home because his back hurt too much to go to work. Then he took to praying. Not just silent little prayers, but loud crying prayers that you could hear all the way down the street. He knelt by his bed, which couldn't have been good for his bad back, but I suppose that was the sacrifice he made to get the Lord's attention, and spent a good part of the day crying and wailing and doing his best to speak in tongues. He thought if he could just "get the Holy Ghost," his problems would be over.

Eventually, he told us he'd "got it," but I don't think he got exactly what he'd expected, because he still had plenty of problems and he didn't seem a bit more holy to me.

Chapter 16

It was about this time that I got the chance to go to church camp. My brother Mitch wanted to go, and I thought maybe I'd try it. Dad didn't seem very happy about it—maybe because he had to pay for it and money was tight. I figured the church probably offered us a scholarship, and Dad had to either bend his pride and take it or come up with it himself. I felt his disapproval for weeks before it was time to go. When I left he said, "Well, if you're going, you'd better get something out of it."

We rode down with Brother James and Sister Annie, who were also taking their boy, Robert, and a couple of his friends. Dear, kind, Brother James. I suspected he had something to do with getting things worked out for me and Mitch to go to camp. Just because Brother James looked like a teddy bear, a big loveable teddy bear, that didn't convince me at all that he couldn't roar upon occasion if need be.

One of those occasions may have been when he discovered my awful insecurities.

Anyone unfortunate enough to have red hair and live in Arkansas at the same time would know what I'm talking about. I went from being called Lucille Ball (and everybody loved Lucy), to Minnie Pearl (with her ridiculous straw hat and dangling price tag), to, (last but not least), Magilla Gorilla. Magilla, the red-haired ape that some kids without enough to do on Saturday mornings liked to watch, was the only identity of the three that offended me. Unfortunately for Brother James, his son Bobby was the principal culprit in tagging me with the moniker, Magilla Gorilla.

Bobby was a crossing guard on Park Avenue when I was in elementary school, and he never missed the opportunity to greet me with, "Morning Magilla," as he swung the cane pole across the street to allow me to cross. I stuck my nose in the air and marched past him like the beetle he was, but I kind of liked it too. At least Bobby noticed me. He knew I had red hair and thought I was worth teasing.

Brother James might have said nothing, might not even have known anything, if Bobby had contented himself with teasing me at the guard crossing. But he was having so much fun with it that he started teasing me at church, too.

One Sunday morning, Brother James came up the steps to the junior high Sunday school department and discovered me hovering on the landing outside the closed door like a bird that can't decide whether to enter the cat's cage or fly away forever.

"What are you doing standing out here, Chelsey?" he asked kindly. It must have been winter because I was visibly trembling.

When I didn't answer, he prodded. "Sunday School has started. Don't you want to go in?"

I nodded and looked away.

"Well . . . " being a patient man, Brother James stood there with me, waiting.

"I . . . can't."

"Why not?" his eyebrows raised.

"Because the boys will tease me."

I saw something flicker in Brother James' brown eyes, something that boded evil for Bobby and his pals.

"Is my boy one of the boys who tease you?"

My silence spoke for itself.

"You tell those boys to go fly a kite!" Brother James said, opening the door.

I went in and sat down, hoping with all my heart that Bobby and the other boys wouldn't hear about the embarrassing scene that just took place outside the door. When I saw the look Brother James threw in his son's direction, I felt torn between two feelings—relief that the teasing might be over, but sad because I was pretty sure that my entry next Sunday would be met with polite silence.

If Brother James was a teddy bear, his wife, Sister Annie, was an angel—his angel, and mine. Her confident smile seemed to say, "It's all right, everything is going to be okay." That smile was a beacon of hope shining through my dark, dark, night.

• • •

It felt good, going off to camp with Sister Annie and Brother James. Unfortunately, I was the only girl in the car so I got to listen to the boys burping and farting all the way there.

They put me in the room with three other girls who came from the same church and I felt like an outcast from the start. They talked about school and parties and sleepovers and all I could think about was, "How is Mitch doing? I hope he makes some friends."

Mitch had a very bad habit of "borrowing" money when he ran out, and that is what got him into trouble at camp. He only had a dollar to make it through the entire week, and being a boy who rarely got the privilege of eating candy or drinking pop, he went wild at the snack shop. A dollar would buy a lot more in those days than it does today, but his money was gone before the week was half over. The boys he borrowed from wanted their money back, and Mitch couldn't give it to them. So they started chasing him and threatening to beat him up. I would have helped him, but by the time he told me, my money was gone, too.

I needn't have feared. Rescue was on the way. Brother James and Sister Annie came to camp on Wednesday night. Since Brother James was a long-time pastor in the Assemblies of God church, he came to camp a lot. I screwed up my courage, swallowed my pride, and asked Brother James and Sister Annie for money. I told them we were out of money and they gave me fifty cents and the same for Mitch.

That put me in a dilemma. I wanted more candy from the snack shop so badly I could taste it. Those long caramel suckers they called Sugar Daddies were the best, and they lasted forever because they were too hard to chew up. Reluctantly, I found my brother and turned the whole dollar over to him. It was worth giving up a sucker to know he would make it home alive.

Meanwhile, camp was not going so well for me either. I seemed to be living in a different world from every other girl there, and I didn't understand their lives any more than they understood mine. I had tried to fit in, I really tried, but I was an ostrich in the midst of eagles.

On the first day of camp, I discovered community showers in the girl's dorm. Since we had only one bathtub with no shower at home, this was a treat for me. The hot water felt good on my body and I liked smelling clean. After my shower I wrapped myself in the big white towel I had brought down with me, just like I had seen the other girls do. I pulled the curtain back and walked to the room. Then I learned what girls do at camp. I heard the three of them running, squealing, down the hallway before they burst into the room. There they "accidentally" dropped their towels and all of them howled in laughter.

I don't know if it was the freedom of being away from home or if eleven-year-old girls just do silly things, but wanting to be part of the crowd and trying to fit in, I dropped my towel, too, and then acted mortified just as they did. And joy of joys, they all laughed. I was in the middle of their laughter. Maybe this camp thing was going to be all right after all. There was a warm feeling deep down under my skin that stayed there through the night and carried me through the next day.

I was feeling so good about the possibility of becoming "one of the girls," that my extraverted nature peeked out from behind the pile of fears I had acquired and I screwed up my courage to talk to the curly-haired evangelist who had talked, sang, and smiled his way into my heart from the platform the night before. He and his petite bride were staying on-site and I knew which cabin was his because I passed it every time I went to the snack shack.

I walked past his door and there he was outside washing his car. It didn't look dirty to me with the sun shining down on it in waves that created a halo effect. This car belonged to a man of God. I thought it should be called the halo-mobile, but that sounded a little corny even to me.

I hesitated a few feet from the car and stood there holding onto my left elbow with my right hand behind my back. He didn't look up at first, so I started to get nervous. Waiting will do that to you sometimes when you are taking a big chance of embarrassing yourself anyway. I dug my toe into the wet red soil and ground out a little hole. Maybe I could crawl into it if this went the way it was starting to look like it would.

Finally he glanced up briefly before looking back down at the spot he was washing with a terrycloth rag.

"Hi," he said. "Can I help you?"

My voice locked up. I didn't expect him to say that. I expected he would say, "Hi, how are you? How do you like my sermons?" So I said the first thing that came to mind.

"I just wanted to tell you . . . " I couldn't remember what I wanted to tell him, so I said, "I like your curly hair."

He smiled but didn't say anything. My heart started going crazy under my rib cage because now I knew I was going to need a bigger hole than the one I had dug with my toe.

After another moment of silence, I said the second thing I could think of, "My uncle has curly hair."

"He does?" the evangelist said. "Is it naturally curly?"

I was puzzled. How could it be curly and not natural? I had never thought about how my uncle's hair came to be curly, I just knew it was. Suddenly, I realized men probably don't have naturally curly hair. So I said, "no."

"Then how does it get curly?" He looked at me with his true-blue eyes, like the color of my blue Crayola. I had never seen eyes that color before.

"Uh . . . his wife rolls it for him."

Now I had the evangelist's undivided attention. He straightened himself up and looked right at me, a laugh playing around his eyes and making them twinkle, with him standing there in the bright sunlight.

"How often does she do that?"

Now I was really in over my head. How should I know how often you have to roll your hair to keep it curly? My first answer had a lucky guess, but I knew I was about to mess up now.

"Every night," I said as if I knew exactly what I was talking about.

At that point the curly-headed evangelist broke into a friendly laugh and I knew I had blown the whole thing. I hurried off without a good-bye and circled the snack-shop without buying anything. I wanted to get back to my dorm and figure out what I had said that was so funny.

I stayed in my room, thinking about it until dinner time. I ate dinner alone, but that was okay because I knew how to make friends with the girls in my dorm. Tonight, I would be the first to drop my towel. I would show them I could be as much fun as anyone. I anticipated the friendly laughter that reached into my inner parts like a stray sun beam in winter as I scrubbed my face and body in the shower. I was first back to the room and first to drop my towel, just as I had imagined.

Everyone stared at me open-mouthed. It was as if I had committed the unpardonable sin. All three girls kind of clustered on one of the girl's bed and started looking at a photo album or something, their backs to me. I got into my pajamas and crawled into bed, covering my head with my sheet to blot out the light and the sound of their giggles and whispered conversation.

You'd think I would have been prepared for the next thing that happened, but I wasn't. A camp counselor came to my room the next day and said she wanted to talk to me. I must have looked apprehensive because my heart started doing double-time. She sat on my bed and told me that the other girls had told her they were uncomfortable rooming with me because I had been doing some bizarre things. I knew she was talking about the towel dropping, but how could I tell her my side of the story without blaming the other girls? Anything I said would sound like a dumb excuse.

Then she said, "Chelsey, has anyone ever done anything to you at home, like . . . touched your privates, or anything?" My face turned so hot I knew it was red as fire, and at the same time a coldness crept up inside me that cut off my words. I managed to deny it, and she left, shaking her head. I turned my face toward the wall and went to sleep.

The next morning I woke up in a circle of pee. This was the second time I had wet the bed and this time I was sure everyone in camp would know about it. Every day at camp stretched into an eternity after that. I wouldn't have made it if it hadn't been for the church services we had at the end of each day. Everyone gathered in the big chapel and listened to a sermon intended to get us saved and filled with the Holy Ghost.

Suddenly, I knew what I needed. I needed the Holy Ghost. If I could just "get it" and speak in tongues, surely God would notice my deplorable condition and do something about it. So I went to the altar, every night. I had no friends to distract me, so I stayed there, begging God to take control of my tongue, night after night. That became the focus of my camp experience.

Now I understood why Dad prayed so hard to get the Holy Ghost. I still remembered when he "got it." He had prayed all day and suddenly started yelling strange words that I couldn't understand. I had closed the door to his room and kept all the kids out so he wouldn't be interrupted. Somehow, it had seemed really important to me that he get what he needed so he could go back to work and live a better life.

Hope came up in me as soon as I hit the altar. Surely, if I prayed hard enough I would get it here. One night it seemed like everyone at the altar was speaking in tongues, so I thought surely this is my night. I'll get it for sure. I stayed there until they started turning the lights off, but it didn't happen. I kept on speaking my words in plain old English. When I got up from the altar, I knew without a doubt that God had passed me by. Yep. He knew everything I had ever done and He wasn't letting me off the hook by wasting his Holy Ghost on me.

• • •

I was glad the boys did their thing on the way home because then no one noticed that I didn't say much. I both dreaded and looked forward to getting home. I wouldn't have strangers looking down their noses at me there, but other things might happen that would be just as bad.

I don't know what Mitch did when he got home, but I went straight to Dad's bedroom. I found him sitting on the bed, his head in his hands, a look of absolute despair on his face. I sat on Mother's bed across from him and tried to ignore the smell of dirty laundry piled up on the floor between us. Somehow the fact that Mother and Dad had separate beds didn't bother me any. Ricky and Lucy Ricardo had separate beds on *I Love Lucy*, so I thought that was the way it was supposed to be.

"Well," Dad looked at me through squinty eyes, "did you have a good time at camp."

"Yeah," I lied.

"Well," he said again. "What did you get out of it?"

His parting words before I left for camp had been running around in my head all week, especially when it came time to go home and I hadn't "got it" yet. If I told him I had a good time, which would be a lie, I knew that wouldn't constitute "getting anything out of it," in his mind. All his hard-earned money and trouble taking care of the younger kids without me there to help out went for nothing if all I did was have a good time.

What I said next surprised me even more that it surprised him. The words that popped out of my mouth came without warning. I didn't have time to think of them, I just opened my mouth and they came out.

"I got the Holy Ghost at camp."

"You did?" He stared at me for a long time and then said, "I hope you're telling me the truth, Chelsey, because those who lie to the Holy Ghost go to hell for it. If you are lying, you better tell me now or you'll probably never get it."

The awful thought of never getting the Holy Ghost and making God really ticked off scared me right down to my toenails. Telling Dad the truth scared me even more so I held on to my lie and started praying every night that God would give me the Holy Ghost so I'd know He hadn't washed his hands of me.

A couple of weeks later I was at church on a Sunday night, praying at the altar. I don't think I was praying for the Holy Ghost right then, but something came over me that was gentle and sweet. It wasn't at all like the ranting sounds Dad had made when he got the Holy Ghost. I felt like someone had wrapped me in a warm blanket on a cold night and took my hand in the dark. I prayed quietly and knew, really knew, that God was listening. Words didn't matter. My lies didn't matter either. My heart grew quiet and felt like a sanctuary for the Almighty.

My Aunt Julie, who was a Nazarene, said I got "sanctified." She said tongues were an outdated way of expressing ourselves and probably offended God. She said if all those girls who spoke in tongues at camp spoke at the same time, they were out of order because only one or two are supposed to speak at once according to the Bible. Aunt Julie knew a lot about the Bible. I think that's why Mother left Dora, my baby sister, with her when we went to Michigan to work the blueberries.

I didn't concern myself much with what Aunt Julie said and I didn't care what those girls had been doing. I knew I had opened my heart to God and He walked into it, and that was enough for me.

Like leprosy, the disease that kills you because you can't feel your pain, those forgotten memories did their work of numbing me up~

Chapter 17

I loved Aunt Julie—admired her too. She was the only blonde in the family and she'd somehow managed to keep her figure. She shared Aunt May's propensity toward an hourglass shape, but it actually looked good on Aunt Julie. Most important, she was young enough to understand me, but old enough to get married and have a house of her own. She loved me too. She told me that when I was little she used to pick me up, braces and all, and carry me around. I was really heavy with all that metal on my legs, but she didn't mind.

I saw a picture of it once, Aunt Julie carrying me around when I was two or three years old, my legs hanging straight down, all encased in steel rods and leather straps. Aunt Julie, who must have been a lot stronger than she looked, was smiling, looking at someone over my head. I think my head was resting on her shoulder, but I can't remember that part for sure.

I'd heard that Aunt Julie was a cancer survivor. She got real sick when she was just a teenager and the doctors told her mama she had leukemia. They never thought she'd live to see twenty. But she did live. Then they said she couldn't get married. But she did get married. "Okay," they said. "Get married, but you'd better not have children. Your body won't stand it." She had children and raised both of them. Aunt Julie never was one to let facts stand in the way of doing what she wanted to do.

I was thrilled when Aunt Julie and Uncle Don, her husband, moved a few blocks down the street from us. I went there as often as I was allowed. Dad liked Aunt Julie, so he let me go a lot. I especially liked our ice cream nights. Aunt Julie and I made a tent out of blankets on her big bed and ate ice cream under it while we talked about girl things. I thought she knew everything.

I liked Uncle Don, too. He teased me a lot about growing up and having boyfriends. That's why I was so disappointed when I heard that he liked little girls. I don't mean "liked," in the way most people do. I mean he liked to spend time alone with them in his bedroom. I heard that Uncle Don did something dirty with Jeannie, my Aunt May's daughter who was only a year older than me. You'd think since Aunt May is my mother's younger sister, Mother and Aunt May would have got together and done something about that, but most people seemed to think the whole thing was Jeannie's fault. She was known to like men a bit more than she ought. But Jeannie wasn't the only girl who found her way into Uncle Don's good graces. Mother said Aunt Julie came home one day and found him in bed with her youngest sister, my aunt Suzy, who was just three years older than me. Suzy was in her early teens at the time, but still looked a lot like Shirley Temple with her round face and dark curly hair. Uncle Don said they were just taking a nap, and Aunt Julie believed him, but she hadn't seen what I saw.

I was there once when Aunt Julie was away at work and Suzy was spending the night. I watched her sit on the couch with Uncle Don's head cradled in her lap, and something about the way he rolled his head around on her legs and whispered to her under the cover of the noise on TV didn't seem quite right. It made my stomach churn like Grandma's old washing machine.

None of that made me dislike Uncle Don, because he was nice to me and usually showed me a lot of attention when Suzy wasn't around.

Then one day something happened that changed the way I thought about Uncle Don. Dad had already made me stop going to his house. Well, he didn't exactly make me. He just pointed out that Aunt Julie treated me special but hurt my brothers' feelings because she didn't invite them down to have ice cream under blankets. It never occurred to me then that the boys wouldn't have wanted to get under blankets with Aunt Julie, and even if they did it wouldn't have been appropriate. I just knew I lost the only friend I had when I couldn't go down there anymore. I missed her and I missed the chance to get out of our house sometimes and talk to someone who didn't live with us.

That's why I was surprised when Uncle Don came by one day and talked to Dad awhile and then, after Dad left for an appointment, told me that I was supposed to come with him to help babysit Aunt May's youngest daughter, my cousin Ruby. I wanted to go because Ruby was so cute at two years old and because I liked Uncle Don. I wanted to get out of the house and do something special and Uncle Don told me he was buying ice cream.

I worried about going. Why did Dad say I could go when he had told me to stay away from Uncle Don? Another relative, Aunt Molly, was in charge of us at that time while both parents were gone, so I asked her, "Did Dad say I could go with Uncle Don?"

"I don't know, hon," she said. "You'd have to ask him."

But I couldn't ask him. We didn't have cell phones in those days and Dad was at an appointment. "Are you sure he said it was okay?" I asked Uncle Don for the dozenth time.

"Of course, I'm sure," he said. "But if you don't want to go . . ."

"Well, if you're sure."

Uncle Don seemed nervous all the time we were shopping. I wondered if he'd had second thoughts about whether Dad would approve of me going with him. He bought lots of good things to eat and tucked Ruby back into the car. But then he did something that surprised me. He took Ruby home. If I was going home with Uncle Don to help him babysit Ruby, why did he take her home before taking me to his house? I started getting that slimy feeling in the pit of my stomach. I didn't want to hurt Uncle Don's feelings, but something just kept telling me to get out of there.

Finally, I said, "Uncle Don, I need to go home." I don't remember him asking me any questions. I think he was thinking that whatever it was he was planning to do for the evening was a really bad idea. He took me home and dropped me off without going in. I saw Dad's Ford Fairlane sitting in the driveway and my stomach started aching. He met me at the door, his face looking like a thunder cloud about to throw-up.

"Where have you been?"

"I went with Uncle Don."

I had hardly got the words out of my mouth before he was unbuckling his belt and yanking it out of his pant loops. That was the part I hated worst. If he had kept the belt hanging on a nail or something so he could just take it down and get the beating over with, it wouldn't have been nearly as bad. Anyone who's had it happen to them will understand that dreaded feeling a child gets when her dad starts tugging at his belt, all the while telling her how bad she's been, and showing her his anger. By the time he had me bent over the bed and my skirt pulled up, I was shaking like JELL-O in an earthquake.

When it was over he made me sit on his bed and his voice got gentle as he explained to me that he just beat me because he loved me and he didn't want something bad to happen to me. He put his arm around me and patted my shoulder. "I know you won't do that again," he assured me.

I nodded, gulping back tears. It was okay that my legs and butt were covered in red welts because Dad loved me. I thought about what Uncle Don had done to Aunt Suzy and felt a little bit proud that I had a dad who wouldn't let that happen to me.

I don't know how I managed to forget the things Daddy had done to me, things that might even have been worse than what Uncle Don did to Suzy, but I think my forgetting might have been a part of some secret plan formulated somewhere in heaven before I was born. Some secrets are just too heavy for children to carry around with them. If they are going to keep walking, and talking, and breathing, they have to figure out how to dump all those awful memories into the deep dark well of forgetfulness. I had done a lot of dumping. The thing is, everything stored at the bottom of that well is subject to being drawn back up someday, maybe when we least expect it, and changing the way we look at all the years in between.

Dad, it seemed, was the only person who loved me enough to take care of me. I determined that I would make sure I wasn't making a mistake next time someone asked me to do something with them. I didn't want to make Dad mad when he was only trying to do what was best for me.

• • •

Maybe that is why I was so quick to say yes when Dad asked me to teach him to read and spell better. He signed up for adult education classes, but still needed some help at home to get through them. Every day when I came home from school, Dad was waiting for me. At first, I felt really special, being Dad's teacher an all, but something started happening soon after that made me dread coming home from school and made me wish I didn't have to be Dad's teacher after all.

Since he was working so hard continuing his education, he seemed to think it was okay to sleep late the next day while Mother went off to work. So he spent some bonding time with me and my siblings in front of the television every night. Maybe Mother didn't notice, but bedtime started getting later and later. He asked me to lie on the couch with him while the other kids sat or lay on the floor beside us. It seemed like a cozy arrangement, especially since I had managed to forget everything that happened before Dustin died. It was like life started "after Dustin" for me. I had managed to blot out everything that made me feel that slimy feeling deep down inside.

Like leprosy, the disease that kills you because you can't feel your pain, those forgotten memories did their work of numbing me up so that I thought Dad was just being a loving Dad when he snuggled up to me on the couch night after night, while John Wayne played the hero on TV until the screen went blank.

I was Princess Salina and I was going to save my people~

Chapter 18

While my external existence just kept getting more complicated, my imaginary life was getting more interesting. Just because my daddy had a strict rule against any of us kids bringing friends home, it didn't mean I didn't have a slew of them—it's just that they lived where nobody else could see them.

Every moment that wasn't dedicated to taking care of my younger siblings, doing all the things Daddy thought had to get done, and immersing myself in the printed word through books and magazines, I was making up my own stories, and I liked them better than most of the ones I read or saw on TV.

One of my favorite TV shows was about a princess who saved her people by throwing herself into a burning volcano. I think her name was Princess Salina. I looked just like her; in fact, after a while, I was her. I was Princess Salina.

• • •

The rain was pouring off the rooftop of our four-foot-by-nine-foot front porch. I sat on the top step, drenched and loving it. My town was under siege. The warring tribe that threatened to destroy us outnumbered us by thousands.

"Princess Salina?" My commander was tall and muscular, with coal black hair and even features. I loved the way he looked at me. My heart raced. I unfolded my slender form and took the hand he offered. It was warm, strong.

"Take me to their leader." I ordered.

I paid no heed to cars passing by on our asphalt street, or the shouts of kids arguing inside our house. I was Princess Salina and I was going to save my people!

I stood before the commander of the enemy forces, straight and serene.

"What are your demands?" I asked.

"Your people have insulted our gods," the commander was quick to reply. "There must be a sacrifice."

Before anyone could speak, before they could stop me, I leaped off the top step of my porch and into the burning inferno.

I wasn't hurt, but Princess Salina was in ashes. Feeling chilled in spite of the hot lava, I went inside and changed my clothes.

Chapter 19

I don't know when we started going to "the country," but it was my favorite thing to do. The country was what we called Grandma and Grandpa Kelsey's farm. It wasn't a real farm, because the only animals were a few hound dogs, but it consisted of fifty acres of Arkansas River low land with an overpopulation of snakes and mosquitoes. It also had an abundance of the biggest clusters of dandelions you ever saw. One time I picked a whole bouquet of them and brought them to my mother. She was in the kitchen with some of her sisters and Grandma Kelsey. I felt suddenly shy when everybody looked at me, the bouquet clutched in my hands.

"I brought you some flowers."

"Oh, honey . . ." Mother handed them back to me, smiling like she always did when she was hanging out with her mother and sisters. "Those aren't flowers, those are just dandelions."

"Oh." I felt the color creep up from my neck to my face and wash over me. I dumped the dandelions, which someone explained to me were nothing more than weeds, on the front lawn.

My cousins, Uncle Bob and Aunt May's kids, lived in a partially-finished house across the street from my grandparents. I liked it there because Uncle Bob raised hunting hounds and I imagined they enjoyed my visits. I felt sorry for the poor things, tied up to trees scattered through the woods all day long. The only time they got off their chains was when they were hunting or competing.

One time we went to a big pig roast where hunters raced their hounds across a red water pond. They tied a big ol' coon to a stake at one end of the pond and started the dogs at the other. In between "king-of-the-mountain" contests, we kids played in the pond. It was mid-summer and the day was a scorcher, so nobody minded the red clay water, almost thick as mud.

The pig was nearly roasted and smelling heavenly when they lined the dogs up for the last race of the day. This time they were going to let the fastest hound get the coon. Everyone lined up on the banks listening to the hounds baying and the handlers hollering. The gun sounded and all those blue-tick hound dogs and red-bone hound dogs plunged into the pond like they were going for broke, and that's when someone noticed a child was in the water. A teenage boy had taken a bet that he could get across the pond before the dogs got to him. I guess he didn't count on the dogs somehow knowing this was their last race of the day, and them smelling that pig roasting and knowing that whoever got there first would get a taste of that coon.

The dogs plowed through the water straight for the prey, just like they'd been taught. My Uncle Terry, Mother's brother, plunged into the pond and swam out to the boy as fast as he could, but by the time he reached him the dogs had already dragged him under. Uncle Terry dived under that red-clay water over and over, searching for the boy. Other men joined him in the water, but no one could find the boy. His mother started wailing and other people were crying. The ambulance came but there was nothing they could do. I don't think anyone ate the roasted pig. Everyone just packed up and went home after that. I heard they dragged the pond the next day and came up with his body. I never did like swimming in ponds after that.

• • •

I was a star at the country just like I had been at harvest camp before I wet the bed. I was a city girl and had culture. That made me alpha girl in the pack and the two cousins closest to my age became my best friends. Unknown to them, they became my only friends.

Aunt May looked a lot like my mother with her chestnut hair and brown eyes, except mother had what she called an hourglass body and Aunt May was a pear. Both of them struggled to keep their weight down—at least they said they struggled—but they weren't winning much because they just kept getting bigger. They said it was us kids that did that to them. Every child, they said, puts about forty pounds on a mother and she'll never lose all of it. When I heard that, I determined then and there that I wouldn't have any children. It wasn't worth the struggle.

Mother, of course, had seven children and Aunt May topped her by one so they had a lot in common. Sometimes they got the whole brood together and took us to a gospel meeting. One such meeting was by Reverend D. J. Spock, who specialized in prophesying.

Reverend Spock was a whole lot of man. I knew he couldn't have borne children, but he had found some other way to get into the struggle because all that weight bulged over his belt and strove at the seams of his suit. He was sweating rivers, which I understood because there wasn't any air conditioning in that tent and it was packed wall to wall with people. There was a sense of excitement that made my red hair frizz up and stand on end.

The meeting started with singing, with Reverend Spock up there cheerleading. His voice punctuated almost every line with "Amen. Sing it children." The cousins and I really got into it, clapping and swinging our hips with the music. I didn't know revival meetings were so much fun.

Maybe one of the reasons I liked it so much was because it was one of the few times Mother took me along with everyone else and Dad didn't come. Uncle Bob didn't come either, so I figured this was a female kind of meeting until I got there and saw bunches of men in suits all waving their hands in the air and shouting right along with Reverend Spock.

Then the Reverend got up to preach. Every other word ended in "and-uh." I thought his round face looked angelic, almost like it was spit-shined from heaven. After a while, Reverend Spock began prophesying. He was picking people out of the crowd and telling them things about their life that he wasn't supposed to know. One lady had cancer but didn't know it. He healed her on the spot. A lean man with a bald spot like a yarmulke on top of his head had just aided in the conception of his fourth child. He hadn't known that yet, so he started rejoicing and the woman beside him stood up and said, "Praise the Lord, Reverend Spock. We've been trying to get that fourth child for seven years now."

"Hallelujah," Reverend Spock said, reaching up to wipe the sweat from his face. "Thank you, Jesus."

Then he pointed to a petite woman in a blue dress sitting about halfway back in the middle row. "You there," he said in his booming voice. "What's your name?"

"Shelia," she said in a trembly voice.

"Shelia," Reverend Spock got serious and a little sad, so I knew he was about to give Shelia bad news, "Your husband is on tour in Vietnam, isn't he?"

Looking like she was staring through a stained glass window, Shelia nodded.

"Please speak up," the Reverend said, "so everyone can hear you."

"Yes," Shelia said. "Yes, he is."

"I regret to tell you this . . . " the Reverend began, and my stomach clenched up. I think I quit breathing, due to the sense of impending tragedy for the pretty little woman who stood with her head cocked to one side, shrouded in fear visible in every line of her body.

The Reverend lowered his voice and spoke close to the microphone, "Your husband is right now in the arms of a Vietnamese woman."

Shelia screamed and ran out of the building, sobbing like there was no tomorrow.

I ducked my head, terror washing over me. If Reverend Spock knew that about Shelia's husband, I wondered what he knew about me.

Just then they started taking the offering and people were shaking their heads, sorrowing over the poor little woman in blue and her unfaithful husband, when Mother said, "Come on, kids. We're getting out of here."

I could have hugged my mother for that. Aunt May gathered up the cousins and we joined the exodus at the back door.

Now, I thought, I know why I didn't see any of the regular attendees of First Assembly of God at Reverend Spock's revival. When they talk about prophesy at First Assembly they usually mean taking the words of the Good Book and trying to figure out what is going to happen to the world—not broadcasting the news of someone's unfaithful husband.

• • •

I loved roaming the woods and exploring the creeks with Aunt May's girls, Darla and Marcie. Darla was my age, a thick, bouncy girl with chestnut hair and bold freckles across her nose. Marcie was one year younger than Darla and me, and prettier than both of us. I thought she looked a lot like my mother—dark-skinned and wide-eyed. We were "sisters." Together we were strong and fearless.

We heard that the cut-up body of a young woman had been found in a sealed barrel in the creek nearest the road. It didn't make it any less scary when we found out she was dead and buried before she was mutilated. Some crazy person had dug her up and kept her in his bathtub for days before he cut her up and put her in the barrel. The kinfolk, which included my parents, Grandma Kelsey, and most of mother's grown-up siblings, agreed that it was probably the work of some perverted Air Force soldier from the nearby base. The only reason they found her is that someone saw the shiny new barrel and thought it would make a nice burning barrel for their backyard. When they took the lid off they saw the body and decided they didn't want the barrel any more.

Real-life stories like that one served to add a tinge of excitement to our excursions into the woods. We were always on the lookout for crazies who might decide to operate on a live girl next time.

One day we followed a deer trail out to the road and came upon a puzzling sight. Cans were lined across the asphalt road like dozens of tin soldiers. The sun reflected off the aluminum tops, flickering bits of blinding light in bright daylight. The two cousins and I stood there in a tight huddle for a while, trying to figure out how so many pop and beer cans came to be lined up across the road. Then a car came around the bend.

The driver slammed on his brakes, nearly throwing his passenger into the dashboard. When he jumped out and slammed the door so hard it shook the entire car, I knew we were in trouble. The soldier—from the Jacksonville Air Force Base—took one look at us and then stomped toward the cousins and me. He was going to kill us. I could tell.

"Let's run!" I yelled and took off for the woods. Darla and Marcie, who always followed my lead, took off after me. We never thought he would chase us through the woods, but he did. All I could hear was crashing foliage and heavy breathing as the four of us played dog and fox through the briar bushes and trees. Somehow I figured out that I wasn't going to outrun our pursuer, not indefinitely, so I headed back for the road. Last thing I wanted was to be caught in the deep woods and mutilated by an angry Air Force soldier like that girl in the barrel. It didn't matter that I was very much alive—he might not care about that.

True to form, the cousins changed direction, too, and all of us met at the road with the soldier right behind us. If I thought he was angry before, it was nothing next to now.

"You wait right here," he said with all his Air Force authority. So we did while he got his pencil and paper out of the car. That's when I noticed a young woman sat up front and a baby was in her lap. She said something to him but he paid her no mind and came back to where we stood all sweaty and trembling.

"Give me your names," he said, stepping up real close to us. "I'm going to report you to the police." Then he started to vent. "I can't believe you could be so stupid. You almost killed my wife and baby, making me slam on my brakes like that. They could have been thrown through the windshield."

When we remained mute he got even madder. "I said, give me your names."

"Don't do it." I told the cousins. They looked bewildered. We were taught to obey adults, and here I was telling them not to mind this angry soldier. What was I thinking?

As if the man wasn't standing right there, Marcie, the youngest and wisest of us, said, "We've got to give him our names. You don't know what he might do to us if we don't."

I shook my head, "No, we can't." I was more afraid of my Dad than the police. I might be okay even if I went to jail, but Dad would never believe my innocence and he would kill me for sure.

Suddenly, the enormity of our predicament, the injustice of being falsely accused, and the marvelous realization that this man would never know if we gave him real names or not, met together somewhere inside my brain and overwhelmed me. I started laughing. At first it was a giggle, and then an outright laugh. Darla caught whatever I had and she started laughing, too. Marcie started crying.

"Don't Chelsey. Stop it, Darla. You are only making it worse."

We could no more have stopped than you can put toothpaste back in the tube. Once we started letting it out, we couldn't control our laughter—it was controlling us. It got worse and worse until finally we were bending over trying to catch our breath between the loud crazy rolls of laughter coming out of our mouths.

We had finally hit on something, even if we didn't mean to, that left the Air Force soldier at a complete loss. He looked at Darla and me laughing our guts out, Marcie crying so hard she was gagging, and said, "You're all crazy." He turned on his heel and stalked back to his car, squealing his tires as he took off down the road.

All three of us girls collapsed beside the road and stared at each other. That's when we heard giggling coming from the bushes across the road and looked over there in time to see Suzy, my mother's youngest sister and Jeannie, the cousin's one-year-older sister, take off through the woods laughing like hyenas. Apparently they had set us up and then stuck around to enjoy the show. I think they got more than even they had bargained for.

• • •

My favorite thing to do, next to exploring the woods, came at nighttime. There were few houses around Grandma Kelsey's farm, and those were occupied by uncles, aunts, and cousins who got up early every morning to feed the hound dogs and begin their workday. So darkness in the country was deeper and thicker than anywhere else I knew, just right for telling made-up stories that would scare the wits out of my cousins.

Our favorite thing to do was gather all the cousins and their cousins who were no kin to me for storytelling. We'd close the door to Grandma's bedroom and sit in a circle on her big quilt-covered bed with all the lights out.

"Bloody bones and butcher knives," I'd say in a low quite voice. "I'm coming to get you!" The little kids squealed and the older ones grinned.

Once I made up a story about an Air Force sergeant who had died in Vietnam and came back in spirit to his old base right there in Jacksonville, Arkansas. I said it was true while crossing my fingers behind my back. The story went like this . . .

> Sergeant Forest O'Daily was a hulk of a man with shoulders like Popeye and a big barrel chest. Why, he once squeezed an enemy to death by human strength alone, in spite of the hatchet the Vietcong carried in one hand and the knife in the other. No enemy in Vietnam was strong enough or smart enough to kill Sergeant O'Daily. Nope, it was a little petite woman in a blue dress who did that. She found out that he had been lying in the arms of a Vietnamese woman, so she got her a ticket to Vietnam. She dressed in camo pants and put her hair up in a cap—then she went hunting for that sorry son of a gun who had done her wrong. She tracked him down like a red-bone hound, smelled him out, and shot him down. Only she didn't use a regular bullet to kill him, she shot him with a silver bullet, 'cause men like O'Daily don't deserve to die a soldier's death—they are blood-sucking vampires who must be put to death with a silver bullet so they won't return and haunt you until you die.
>
> Well, as it turns out, Sergeant O'Daily was innocent. He never slept in the arms of that Vietnamese woman like Reverend Spock said. The Vietnamese woman was a nurse and

O'Daily was injured in battle. The woman in blue realized too late what she had done, so she turned the gun on herself and took the second bullet. What she didn't know was that silver bullets work to keep vampires dead, but do the opposite on pure-blooded men and women. They keep their spirit alive even when their body is dead.

So the woman in blue and her beloved husband made up and came home to America. They didn't need to fly on a plane because spirits can go anywhere they please. They came right back to Sergeant O'Daily's home base in Jacksonville, Arkansas and took to looking for the Reverend Spock. Everyone who had gone to his tent revival took on a little of his smell, so they'd better watch out that O'Daily and his woman don't mistake them for one of Spock's followers and come after them.

Be careful of the night, 'cause spirits hunt after dark. Don't get too close to trees, buildings, or cars because spirits like to hide behind them and jump out to get you when you're not looking . . . .

The best part of my storytelling came when one of the older kids could sneak out of the room without being noticed and hide behind the very objects I had mentioned. They'd wait until the young ones got close enough to touch, and jump out yelling like banshees. Then we'd all sit back and laugh about it together. None of us wanted to stick around outside to enjoy our little joke, and we carefully avoided the trees and buildings as we went back inside until time for the cousins to go home.

They went in a bunch because no one wanted to go home alone. That's when I decided I might want to be a writer when I grew up.

I would not let her see me cry even if the tears welled up like a giant wave inside and drowned me~

Chapter 20

There were multiple talents in my family. Dad played the guitar, and he taught Mitch and O'dell how to play. I liked country music and hymns, but my brothers preferred rock. All of us liked to write our own songs and sing them for everyone we knew.

Before long, I was taking Mitch and O'dell on long walks and asking neighbors if we could come in and sing for them. I even learned how to strum a few bars on the guitar and every one of us could sing. Once we went to "the projects" to play for an elderly couple who were down on their luck. They made us fresh lemonade and smiled until I thought their faces would crack. They lived in a four-room house that had been put up on cinder blocks and renovated in the urban renewal project. Dad had sold them the house and they believed he was a direct answer to their prayers. When he told them that he and his kids sang gospel songs, they invited us to come do a gospel singing at their house. I felt like a regular star as I harmonized into the microphone with my brothers while a crowd gathered outside the front door. There was lots of singing and clapping going on outside as well as inside and we went home exhausted but happy when it was all over. I heard the neighborhood talked about it for weeks.

The success must have gone to my head because I decided I'd like to be on the Tommy Trent show. I was going to be a real-life singing star. I asked mother to take me down to audition with Mr. Trent at the Tommy Trent Fun Barn on Pike Avenue, and she did it. I went in with my guitar intending to sing "I cheated my baby," a song I had written and had put to music, but lost my nerve the minute I saw Mr. Trent. He was a middle-aged man with an oversized belly and a nice smile that should have reassured me. But he was also a television man, someone with the power to make a star out of me—or not.

"Okay, kid," he said. "Let's see what you've got."

It's now or never, I thought. I hooked my guitar over my shoulder and started strumming. I was mortified when no music poured out of the strings. Looking down, it took a moment to register that I had my guitar turned around so that the strings were against my stomach and I was strumming the back of the guitar. I must have blushed a dozen shades of pink before I managed to get the guitar turned around. Mr. Trent held up his hand.

"I don't think you're quite ready for the show," he said. "Why don't you come back in a couple of years and give it another try."

I nodded and left the "thank you" up to mother as I sheepishly headed for the door. Call me a glutton for punishment, but that wasn't the end of my singing career. I had more embarrassments headed my way. I tried out for the Junior High Ensemble.

The music department had about one hundred and fifty kids but only eight would be selected to represent the school in the ensemble. Imagine my surprise when I was actually chosen.

"How much extra time do you have to spend at the school to be in this?" Dad asked when I shared my good news.

"I don't know." I hadn't really thought about it.

I thought he would be proud, but he seemed a little mad. That wouldn't have been so bad, but every time I had to stay over at school to practice, I felt like I must be doing something wrong because Dad was always in a bad mood when he came to pick me up. I missed several practices because I was needed at home. I can't remember why, I just knew I couldn't go.

After weeks of practice, we finally got to go to a school in another area and show off our stuff. We got lots of praise and applause for our performance and I came back feeling, for the first time, like I had found where I really fit in. Unfortunately, I happened to share the seat on the bus with a fellow student of the opposite sex.

When I got in the car with Dad, I knew something was terribly wrong. He was furious.

"See, I knew this music thing was just a way for you to get together with boys. I saw you sitting by that boy when the bus drove up."

Somehow I ended up confessing that I did enjoy sitting by the boy in my class on the trip home and, yes, we did talk some. I apologized over and over but that didn't appease Dad's anger.

"I just can't trust you," he said.

I offered to quit the ensemble—anything to stop the hostility that escalated when Dad was mad.

"Maybe you should," he said, sounding a little sad that it was necessary for me to quit. "If it's going to lead you down the wrong road to sing in this thing then it's better if you just get out of it."

I told Mrs. Jones, my music teacher, that I was going to have to quit the ensemble.

"Good," she said. "You haven't been faithful to practice anyway and I'd rather have someone in your place who appreciates the honor of singing in our school ensemble."

She didn't see me cry because I held back the tears with an iron resolve. I would not let her see me cry even if the tears welled up like a giant wave inside and drowned me. I grieved for a long time after that, dealing with a loss beyond my comprehension. Slowly, quietly, I was losing myself and becoming an extension of someone else—someone whose love and affection came at a price I was barely beginning to understand.

Chapter 21

I still can't quite figure out what happened to my memories. It's like I took a big old blotter about the size of my brain and stamped everything out that made that horrible slimy feeling come up. In the process, I stamped over everything good along with it, leaving a burned out hole where my memories should have been.

I'm certain there were some good times with my siblings that I wanted to remember. Surely, when I came home from Aunt Judith's house and discovered my newborn sister, I enjoyed holding her, maybe giving her a bottle, or playing with her. Even before that, it seems like I'd remember something about Mother bringing home the "blue baby," since most four-year-old girls play with their baby brother and make a few memories. Shouldn't I also remember something about Mitch, since he was only two years younger than me?

Someone told me later that a thing called "trauma-induced amnesia" was responsible for the loss of my memories, but it seems to me like I just slept-walked through a good part of my life.

I must have woke up at about twelve, because I remember a lot of things that happened after that. Maybe that's how long it takes to grieve your brother when you know you had your part in killing him.

• • •

I was about twelve when my imagination decided to take a turn for the worse. Maybe it had something to do with the hormones invading my organs, but I learned to create a life for myself that no one could take away from me—because every bit of it took place in my mind.

Occasionally, my adolescent imagination gave me cause for unexpected embarrassments.

My favorite television show at twelve was *Bonanza*, primarily due to my attraction to Little Joe Cartwright. He was a perfect gentleman and cute as could be. I wanted him to kiss me, but good girls don't go around letting boys kiss them, so I had to resist. I discovered my siblings could be counted on for prop acting, which made my fantasies come true—at least in my own mind.

One day I was out in the backyard, half hidden by the forsythia bush which had exchanged its golden flowers for a wealth of glossy green leaves. Little Joe was out there with me, begging me to marry him. *I can't*, I told him, *my Dad will never allow it.* He grabbed my hand (at this part I grabbed my own hand) and pulled me to him.

"Don't, Little Joe," I begged, though of course I didn't mean it. Just then I looked up, straight into the amused eyes of my next-door neighbor—the one who fondly called himself Doc Holiday. I tucked my head and walked sedately back to the house, refusing to look back in his direction. I heard his chuckle from the back door. Let him laugh. Little Joe opened the door for me and we both went inside.

I soon forgot Doc's laughter and returned to my theatrics in the backyard. One day a delightful wind was blowing and I began twirling. Faster and faster I whirled myself around with my eyes closed. I imagined the wind sweeping me into the sky where I continued to pirouette all the way to the clouds. I still dream, sometimes, of flying on the wings of the wind with the cool breezes of early summer blowing through my hair. I never want to stop dreaming until the day comes that I fly away on the breath of God, never to return to the earth again.

I kept thinking about Aunt Molly's three eyed infant and thanking God that I wasn't going to be another family abnormality~

Chapter 22

Lots of things change when you turn thirteen. One of my changes was getting a bump on the left side of my chest. It hurt like a boil, but didn't look infected. In fact, it was right underneath my flat pink nipple. It scared me enough to send me running to Mother.

"Let me see," Mother said. She looked at it and then felt it. I winced and jerked away from her. She took me to the doctor for a diagnosis. Dr. White's clinic had burned down, so we had a different family doctor, named Dr. Smith.

Dr. Smith examined me and then put on his best doctor voice and said, "That's just your breasts coming in."

"But doctor," I said. "I thought you were supposed to have breasts (I winced at the word) on both sides."

He smiled ever so slightly, and said, "You are, but they don't always come in at the same time. The soreness will go away in a few months."

I went home both chagrined and relieved. *I'll bet I'm the only girl in Arkansas who goes to the doctor to be told she's developing breasts,* I thought. At least I'm gonna get two of them and that proves I'm normal. I kept thinking about Aunt Molly's three-eyed infant and thanking God that I was not going to be another family abnormality with only one breast on my developing body.

Other changes were taking place, too. Unexpected and scary as they were, I welcomed them because they, too, meant I was like other girls—at least in those ways.

I was in geography class the next time I found out how normal I was. The teacher had asked me to come write something on the blackboard. I had just finished it and was returning to my seat when a girl in the front row whispered, "Chelsey," and beckoned for me to come close so she would whisper in my ear.

"You've got blood on the back of your dress."

Without missing a beat, I said, "Oh, no, that's just ketchup." When the girl kept looking at me without blinking, I said in a louder voice, "I sat in ketchup in the cafeteria. That's what I got on my dress." Still, my cheeks flamed as I returned to my seat, trying to ignore the deafening quiet in the large class of sympathetic students.

Another sensitive soul whose efforts to help me changed the course of my life was Sister Jackie Bowman. She taught my seventh-grade Sunday school class. One day she gave every girl in her class a book about the inner beauty of a woman by someone who should know, Miss America. I devoured every word of it. That's when I decided I should get my hair cut.

Chapter 23

Actually, I didn't want to get my hair cut, I just wanted to be able to comb through it. My semi-curly hair was long and thick. It was also matted with dirt, old hairspray, and tangles. I tried to straighten it out at home but couldn't get a comb through it. I asked Mother if I could go to the beauty shop for a cut and she said yes. I went to a downtown salon in a rather old part of Little Rock, and got more than my money's worth. Not only did they cut my hair, they had me pose for pictures.

A middle-aged man did the cut and then put me in the chair for photos. I was wearing a slimming shift that barely reached my knees, a welcome improvement from the mid-shin dresses I had worn in grade school. He said the salon worked with modeling scouts and they wanted to provide a picture of me to the scout. Something about the way he touched my leg when he spun me in the chair felt awkward and unnatural. The way other hair stylists looked at me, almost as if they were jealous or a little mad, sent my "alert" system to orange. I let them take the pictures because I was afraid to say no, and then got out of there, all the while looking behind me. I was certain I was about to be abducted and sold off to some prostitution ring down in Florida or somewhere.

• • •

I began washing my hair often and brushing it every day. I used acne medication and special soap to clear my complexion. I began to look into the mirror, just like Miss America said she did, and tell myself, "You are beautiful." I didn't have to believe it, I felt better just because I had permission to say it. I didn't want to be vain, but Miss America herself gave me permission to do it, so it had to be all right.

About that time, I found out Mother was pregnant again. Something was different this time. I began to look forward to the baby coming. I wanted to hold him and rock him. I dreamed of singing songs to him and helping take care of him. My maternal instincts had kicked in and that gave me a purpose to live.

The day Willy was born, I was so proud. I made up a big sign that said, "It's a boy!" and asked a teacher to pin it to my back.

"Are you sure you want to wear this?" She asked. I ignored the concern in her voice and nodded yes. I was sure.

I wore the sign around all day and was completely surprised when someone told me they thought I had given birth to a baby. Couldn't the idiots see that I was flat as a board? I had watched my mother's belly swell, as well as her legs and arms and everything else, during this pregnancy. What did they know if they thought I could have gone to school with them everyday carrying a fully-developing baby? I didn't let it bother me. I had a baby brother and no one was going to steal my joy!

I think it was about this time that we got Donald. Donald was a marvel and a wonder. He was better than any dog and he knew it, too. Of course, he had to be rescued first.

I went out into the backyard and found him (O'Dell) standing over an open grave with a shovel still in his hand~

Chapter 24

It was just after Easter and the boy across the street had got a little yellow duck, a real one, as an Easter present. He showed off by throwing the poor little thing into the air and catching it as if it was a ball. O'dell yelled at him to stop. The boy laughed and plunked the duck into a kiddie pool, poking it from behind to make it swim. When he finished scooting him around in the pool he took him out and put him on the ground. The duckling fluttered his small wings and tried to get away. It was enough to make a grown man cry seeing that little thing waddling along, trying to hold his head up.

O'dell had had enough. He grabbed the duckling and stomped away with it, ignoring the boy's wail.

O'dell brought it home and gave it to me. I cuddled the small warm body in my hands, honored to be entrusted with the task of nursing it back to health.

After a couple of hours, the mother of the boy showed up at our door. O'dell, full of the wisdom of his ten years, went to meet her.

"You have my son's duck," the mother said.

"I sure do," O'dell said.

"Well, you better give it back."

"He ain't gettin' it back."

"I'm gonna call the cops!" She threatened.

"Go ahead," O'dell stood right in her face. "I'll show 'em what he did to it and let's see what they say about that."

The woman turned in a huff and walked back across the street and we never heard any more about it.

• • •

Perhaps our neighbor had heard about O'dell's latest mishap in the neighborhood. O'dell was only ten years old, but he had an intense love affair with Rebecca Holmes. It lasted almost a year before Rebecca's dad decided O'dell wasn't good enough for his daughter and made her tell O'dell she couldn't see him anymore.

Rebecca's house happened to back right up to our favorite creek—actually, just a drainage ditch. One day O'dell was crossing the bridge that spanned the creek, hoping for a glimpse of his true love, when he saw Rebecca. Unfortunately, she wasn't alone. Another boy about her age was hugging on her at the creek's edge. The boy looked up and saw O'dell staring, rage stitched into every line of his body, and hollered, "What you looking at, you *$#* fool?" Obviously, this boy didn't know O'dell.

O'dell jumped off the bridge, right onto that boy's back and started pumping his fists into him. The boy screamed and bawled for his mother. Since she lived in the house a few doors down, she heard him and came running. She pulled O'dell off her boy and asked, "What'd you do that for?"

O'dell, full of righteous fury, said "Your boy called me a #$@* fool."

The mother turned and looked at her boy, who by now had fixed his gaze on the brown water of the creek. "Well, did you? Did you say that?" His silence told her all she needed to know.

"Get on home!" She shouted, giving her son a little push in the right direction.

She left, shaking her head, and O'dell took one last look at Rebecca before he moseyed on home, gratified to see tears in her eyes. The magic was still there.

• • •

Naming the duckling was a family project. By mutual agreement we christened him Donald. I fed him, held him, and slept with him on my pillow. One day when he was much better, I filled the bathtub with water and let him swim around in it.

When he was bigger and the weather grew warm, I took Donald outside. The other kids began playing with him, giving him all the respect he deserved. As he grew big and strong, Donald became quick as well.

The first time Donald joined us for a ball game in the backyard, we were all amazed. We were half throwing, half rolling a nine-inch, brightly-colored ball to each other, going around a circle. Someone started the ball rolling and Donald launched himself after it. He ran with all his might, flapping his wings and squawking until he connected with the ball. Everyone broke out in a fit of laughter when Donald strutted around the circle as if to say, "Yeah, look at me. I'm the best!" Soon after that, I gave the duck to my brother O'dell, because he wanted to be a veterinarian and I knew he would take good care of him.

Dad didn't care much for animals, but he tolerated Donald because he was a lot less trouble than a dog, and six kids occupying a 50- by 140-foot lot with a fenced-in yard needed something to keep them busy. But Donald almost lost his position as the family pet when he got too proud of his dominance one day and overstepped his bounds.

The boys, Mitch and O'dell, had the unpleasant job of taking the garbage out to the rusted barrel at the back of the yard a couple of times each week. That had been Dustin's job, but it fell to the younger boys when Dustin went on to his eternal reward. Unlike Dustin, Mitch and O'dell didn't always follow the rules. They were half-mad at Dad most of the time for beating them or taking away precious privileges. I think resentment had more to do with what happened next than laziness.

They started putting the garbage under the crawl space instead of carrying it to the barrel. We noticed an increase in roaches, but didn't know the cause of it. Then one day we had a plumbing problem. Someone called the plumber. Being a friendly sort, he volunteered to go under the house and check out the source of the problem. He didn't know what he was getting himself into.

After spending a few minutes in our crawlspace, he came to the door red-faced and sweaty. In words I can't repeat here, he informed Dad that our crawlspace was a stinking garbage heap occupied by vermin of the filthiest sort, and that he could sue us for the malicious attack on his person by our mentally-deranged duck. Apparently, Donald saw the plumber as an imposter and took it on himself to rid our premises of the perceived menace.

We kids were secretly proud of Donald, but promised to make sure he was locked up if another plumber came to call. Mitch took it upon himself to improvise a chicken-wire coop for Donald and he had his own little bowl of water which O'dell faithfully filled to the brim every single day. Donald had a dog's life and he loved it.

Meanwhile, the roaches continued to increase their population in our house from their fertile breeding ground underneath it. One day, Dad decided the only way to correct the problem was to put out roach poison. To keep the kids out of it, he planned a trip to Newport to visit Aunt Judith.

"Be sure you lock that duck up real good," he told the boys. "If he gets into the poison, it will likely kill him."

We went off to Newport for the week end and came back late Sunday evening. We were all exhausted and went straight to bed. The next morning, I couldn't find O'dell when it was time to leave for school. I went out into the backyard and found him standing over an open grave with a shovel still in his hand. He was crying so hard it broke my heart. Then I saw Donald. He was lying beside the grave with a big black water-bug poking through a hole in his bill. He had devoured so many of the poisoned bugs that it ate through his beautiful orange bill. I could only imagine what it did to his stomach. O'dell placed Donald in the freshly dug grave and covered him over with dirt, packing it level with the ground around it. He went off to school and grieved silently. I grieved too, not only for Donald but for my little brother who bore his grief alone.

...the need to care for my siblings was probably the one thing that kept me alive during those days~

Chapter 25

Since Mother spent most of her time at the real estate office, I did the cleaning, laundry, and childcare while she was gone. Some would say I shouldn't have had so much responsibility, and they would be right, but the need to care for my siblings was probably the one thing that kept me alive during those days.

Besides, I adored them. Dora was only three when Willy was born and I was always taking her picture. There must be something common about little girls and fancy panties because Dora had a pair of white panties with bright red letters that said, "I'm the Boss," written right across the butt. She loved to show them off and get her picture taken.

My favorite was the one of her bending over in front of the forsythia bush on a dazzling summer day. Her towhead shone like spun gold beneath the afternoon sun and the grin on her face reached from ear to ear. She looked right into the camera with her emerald eyes as if daring anyone to dispute her claim.

• • •

Somehow, even at the young age of thirteen, I knew kids had to get out of the house and have some fun or else go crazy, so I put Willy in a stroller and gathered up the rest of the kids—Mitch, O'dell, Suzanne, and Dora—and off we went to "explore" our neighborhood. We took long walks along the railroad track, explored the culvert underneath it, and stopped to talk to neighbors, some of whom started calling me the "little mother."

Then there was the creek. Actually, the creek was a drainage ditch, but you'd never know it. Dustin had caught catfish and crawdads in it. He learned to respect catfish because their sharp fins would not only poke you, but inject some kind of toxin into your skin that stung like heck. I showed the boys how to pick up crawdads and all of us got some relief from the hot summer sun by getting wet in the shallow water of the ditch.

One day in early spring, the ditch nearly claimed my sister Suzanne. Spring run-off could raise the water level from a few inches to five or six feet in a matter of hours as all the lowlands around our area drained into it. We lived fairly close to the Arkansas River, so the ditch didn't have to conduct its torrents very far to empty out into the treacherous currents of the river. It had rained for days, flooding the yard across the street from our house and getting into the houses. Seven-year-old Suzanne was nowhere to be found, so Mother went looking for her. Her first thought was the ditch. Sure enough, when she got there she found Suzanne standing on the bank staring into the brown swirling water. Her long red hair swirled around her face in the quiet breeze, her face blanched white as a peeled almond. Spine straight, she stood like a mature oak tree, entranced by the wind and the water and something else that no one could see except Suzanne. Mother got to her in time and drew her back from the edge of the water. She always suspected that our nearest neighbor, Doc Holiday, had something to do with Suzanne's fixation on the violent creek, but she never told me what that "something" was.

I had seen Suzanne stare at other objects with the same intensity that she focused on the swirling water of the ditch. Sometimes when Dad and Mother were arguing or Dad was punishing one of the kids for some misbehavior, Suzanne could be seen staring at a hole in the wall as if it was a magic looking-glass through which she could escape the misery of the moment if she could just figure out how to get on the other side of it. She also stared at flies on the wall, pictures, and windows without blinking or speaking. I guess that was just her way. I had mine as well.

Suzanne tried to escape what she couldn't control by squeezing her mind into a pinhole on the wall or some other object, while I tried to fix the problem. I thought escape was impossible. I could have run away, but by now I had become "little mother," and I couldn't take my children with me.

Something that felt like a three edged stone kept turning over and over, digging into my happiness~

Chapter 26

In the seventh grade, I met Phyllis Miller. She lived in a two-bedroom bungalow about six blocks from me. Her house was always full of family and friends. My definition of friends at that point was "anyone who wants to spend time with you." That's why acceptance came easy with Phyllis. I was as welcome as anyone. Problem was, some of the friends she welcomed into her house, and the activities she ordained, were less than desirable, if you know what I mean.

One of them was a sixteen-year-old boy. He wanted me to date him, whatever that meant. I felt pretty proud. After all he had his own car, a Corvair. If you remember those little coupes, then you know it would have been hard to squeeze more than two people into it. I got it mixed up with a Corvette and told everyone, except my Dad, of course, that a boy who hung out at Phyllis' house wanted to take me out in his Corvette. As soon as my brother, Mitch, saw the old rust bucket with its many coats of patched up paint, he informed me, "It ain't no Corvette. It's a stupid Corvair."

I didn't care. A boy with a car and lots of friends liked me and wanted to take me out. He even had a favorite song that he said was "our song." It was all so romantic, it made me love him on the spot. I think I even sat in the car with him a couple of times while he played "our song" on the radio. He was so deep. It was just like he was a poet who wrote the words to our song, since he liked them so much.

I don't remember much of the song, but I'll never forget the message. It was about a boy who lived "down in the boondocks." He was hopelessly in love with a girl (like me), but he couldn't date her because he "doesn't fit in her society."

So romantic! Most people didn't think of me as a member of high class society. His sentiments went straight to my head.

I wanted to go out with this kid, though I don't remember his name now, and I tried to figure out how I could make that happen without my Dad knowing about it. Something down inside me, something that felt like a three-cornered rock, kept turning over and over, digging into my happiness. It never stopped and all that bleeding inside finally made me fess up to what I had been doing.

"I met a boy at Phyllis' house," I told my Dad. I couldn't handle the guilt anymore. I knew only bad girls went out with boys behind their Dad's back and I wanted to be a good girl. I thought I deserved Dad's scorn when he looked at me all disappointed and upset.

"What did you think you were going to do when you 'went out with him?'" Dad's lips curved into a scowl on those last four words and I looked down.

"I don't know."

"You need to answer me!"

"Uh, let nature take its course, I guess." Where had I heard those words? In a song I think, but I had no ideas where nature might lead, and my Dad seemed to think it led only one place.

"You stay away from that boy and that girl, Phyllis. Do you hear me?"

I nodded, feeling an emptiness inside. Why bother to make friends? It always turned out like this.

I stopped going to Phyllis' house and counted myself lucky that I had narrowly escaped the course of nature. But I couldn't give up her friendship. Phyllis and her friends sat with me at lunch. They talked to me. They kept me from being alone at school. I was finally a part of something bigger than myself, a teen-aged gang.

I didn't know that's what they were, but when Phyllis started inviting me to skip school with her and go to empty houses to have some fun, I was terrified by my own indecision. I wanted to go, not for the fun really, but to keep up my part of the friendship. Then she said they had some booze, sometimes they even had some pot, and that was too much for my fragile conscience. No way was I going to go that far down the forbidden path. I wanted out.

There was one problem with that. While it was easy to get into Phyllis' gang, it was hard to get out. She and her friends had already managed to beat up two other kids who tried to get out of their little group. I knew a beating, or worse, would happen to me if I separated myself from them. My only hope lay in making them afraid of me, and how was I doing to do that? I had never been in a fight, never been the menacing type, unless you count the mean looks I had learned to give my teachers.

Having no one else to turn to in my dilemma, I turned to God. First Assembly was having a revival. I went on a Wednesday night. When the preacher gave the altar call, inviting everyone who was struggling with sin to come up front and lay their burdens at the altar, I went forward. Something happened there that night that I can't explain, but I know it gave me strength to do what I had to do.

I was standing there at the front of the church with a whole line of other people—people whom I thought were holy men and women. I was surprised, at first, to know that they had sins, too. Then, something happened that made me forget all about them. A strange sensation came over me, settling like a soft silk skirt over my head and down onto my body. All of a sudden, my feet were on fire. I pictured red hot coals coming up to my ankles, burning, burning all the way to my knees. I started stomping, fast and furious, trying to put out the fire. Finally, my feet cooled and I felt a peace sitting on my shoulders that hadn't been there before.

Some folks might say religion had just offered me a catharsis for my pent-up emotions and that's why I felt so serene after it was all over. Aunt Julie said that just like Isaiah had a coal from the altar laid on his tongue so God could cleanse his words and make him a prophet, God cleaned up my feet so I could get off the wrong path and grow up to lead others to him, just like the Prophet Isaiah.

All I know is I left church that night knowing I had to get out of Phyllis' gang even if it killed me, and I was prepared to die if I must.

So the next day, before I could back out of it, I followed Phyllis home from school. She had a buddy with her, but that didn't keep her from speeding up and keeping a distance between us. Every time she looked back I gave her the same glare that worked on Mrs. Atkins, and felt a little thrill when she looked scared witless.

All the way home, I thought of what I could say to pick a fight with her and make it stick. It had to be something that I couldn't take back later if I got tempted to renew my old friendship. Phyllis may have thought she was running, or practically running, from me, but I didn't want to catch her either. Not yet. I had a solid sense of propriety that kept me from making a public spectacle of myself. I kept searching for a private place to do what I had to do.

That didn't happen until Phyllis made it all the way home. She stepped into her own yard and dropped her books. "You want me, come get me."

I advanced slowly, not relishing for one minute what I was about to do.

"Why are you being such a jerk?" She yelled, loudly enough to bring her family out to the porch. They started yelling and swearing at me, too, but nothing could deter me now. I had my story made up.

"You wrote, 'Chelsey's mother is a bitch,' on the bathroom door, that's what." I yelled back at her.

"I did not." She protested her innocence, but took a step toward me.

I don't know who threw the first punch, but suddenly we were on the ground, hands balled into fists, swinging and rolling in the dirt. I heard whistles and cat calls and realized my quest for privacy had been in vain. Several men on top of a nearby building dropped their roofing shingles and nails to egg us on.

Phyllis' mother screamed, "You get out of here or I'm going to call the cops!"

I had done it. I walked the rest of the way home in a daze. I was out of the gang for sure, but who could know the price I'd have to pay for it.

I arrived home a few minutes later with a quarter-size bruise on my cheek, bits of grass sticking up in my hair, and a tear in my dress. Dad was always telling the boys how to fight, things like drawing a line in the dirt and spitting over it, so I knew he'd be proud of me for taking care of myself. He looked up when I came in the door.

"What happened to you?"

"I got in a fight with Phyllis."

"Did you hurt her?" He eyed the darkening bruise on my left cheek.

"I don't think so." My answer precipitated a long lecture about how to fight and make it count. Guess I didn't make him proud after all.

I went to school the next day with a sharp sense of dread. Then I saw Phyllis. My little bruise was a speck next to her big shiner. Her entire right eye was an ugly purple and swollen completely shut. Best of all, she wouldn't even look at me. A sense of safety overwhelmed me then and I gave thanks to God for answering my prayers. I was out of the gang.

I worked hard at trying to be good after that, and hoped that somehow my efforts would make everything better for me and my siblings. It didn't, so I had to learn other ways to get the job done. One day at a time, I learned how to manipulate my environment to protect those I loved most—my sisters and brothers. I didn't know until many years later that it was the other way around. I was being manipulated by a force that would drain every ounce of life out of me and leave me as empty as the dried-up carcasses of the bugs that sipped Dad's poison in their futile effort to survive.

• • •

We had taken to going to Newport to spend Christmas with Aunt Judith and my dad's cousins. He'd grown up with some of Aunt Judith's kids. Since she'd had thirteen of them over a period of several decades, the older ones were his age and the youngest were closer to my age.

One of his cousins was the ugliest woman I've ever seen. I'm not trying to be mean, but she resembled a Neanderthal man. I might think more of her if she hadn't decided to move in with us and, well . . . I'll get to that later.

Another cousin, Timmy, lived in St. Louis and came home sometimes for Christmas. I liked him. Another cousin, Buddy, usually showed up as well, along with his wife and kids. He's the one who had given me that cherished Almond Joy so many years back. That's why I went along when Dad drove Aunt Judith and the twins up to Illinois to comfort his cousin Timmy after his family got in a terrible accident on the way home to St. Louis. His wife had gone to sleep at the wheel and nearly killed the whole family.

• • •

Who am I kidding? I didn't go because I liked Dad's cousin or cared about his family. I went because Daddy expected me to. I don't know how I knew this, but I knew. I always knew.

When we got to the hospital, Buddy was already there. I think he was glad to see me. We learned that one of Timmy's sons was dead and his wife and other son were in danger of dying, too. I felt sad for them, but not too much, for I don't think I was feeling much of anything about that time. Something was happening that I can't quite remember, or I didn't even understand, but I think it had something to do with what happened next.

Dad told me I was going to share a hotel room with him—alone. I remember the feelings more than the happenings. Sickened, sad, embarrassed, afraid, alone. Afraid enough to talk to Aunt Judith.

"I want to stay with you and the girls."

I don't remember Aunt Judith as an extremely perceptive person, but something came up in her that day that made me love her. She told my Dad that I was staying with her and her girls—and that was the end of it.

But Dad, never one to give up his pride, found a way to make me pay for my momentary rebellion. He had me meet him at the elevator the next morning. I think he had roomed with Buddy the night before, because Buddy was standing at the elevator with him. But Buddy wasn't going up—or down—or wherever Dad was going with me, so Daddy and I got on the elevator alone.

That's when Dad paid me back for my small defiance the night before. I don't remember what he did, but I knew it was bad, because I never felt proud of myself around Buddy after that, and he never really talked with me or looked me full in the face either.

When Buddy was getting his affairs in order for his impending death several decades later, he called my mother to bare his chest. He had been carrying his sadness for over twenty years but couldn't take it to the grave with him.

He told mother that he saw my daddy pull up my skirt after he stepped onto that elevator. He couldn't believe what he had just seen because my daddy was such a fine upstanding man. So he tucked that information away in the back of his mind and tried to forget about it for more than twenty years.

You didn't mean to wrong me, Cousin Buddy. I wish you could have told someone what he did, but it wouldn't have made much difference. Both of my Grandmothers told my mother their suspicions on three separate occasions, and it didn't change anything. One of my grandmothers told my mother because she thought I should be protected; the other told her because she was indignant that I was treading on my mother's territory. No one told me anything until I figured out on my own how to get out of the whole horrible mess. And that would take a long time.

Mother didn't tell anybody. If I didn't cater to my daddy's whims, our whole family just might fall apart. She told me later that she couldn't stand the idea of being in poverty, and how could she provide for six hungry kids? Besides, she said, she loved my Daddy and she couldn't believe he would really do anything to hurt me.

If I had known the price I would pay for my two hours of freedom, I would have run all the way home the moment the bell rang~

Chapter 27

Junior High was a lonely place for me. I began to eat lunch in the school cafeteria with a girl named Laura. Laura didn't have any friends either, so we had at least one thing in common. One day I went to school and learned soon after arriving that there was a teacher's conference in early afternoon, so we would be released from classes two hours early. I dreaded going home. I knew Dad would be there alone, because he always stayed home when his back hurt and it had been hurting a lot lately. So I was relieved when Laura said she didn't want to go home either and why didn't we just hang out and have some fun? Something inside me told me not to do it, but something else told me it was worth taking the risk of being found out. If I had known the price I would pay for my two hours of freedom I would have run all the way home the minute the bell rang.

It was great fun having a friend. I felt kind of like a normal teenager. I was doing something exciting and daring, and moreover I was doing it with another girl my age. I didn't begin feeling that sinking fear until Laura left to go home and I started my own journey homeward. I walked the railroad tracks as I always did, my feet moving slower by the moment as I neared my house. When I turned the corner on my street my worst fears were confirmed. Dad was home and he was standing on the porch, rage sticking out on every line of his body. I couldn't look at him as I walked across the yard. I squeezed past him at the door, my head down.

He followed me inside and the interrogation began. He made me sit on Mother's bed across from him while he alternated looking at me with those angry, disappointed eyes and demanding to know where I was and what I was doing for a whole two hours after school.

I told him the truth. "Laura and I walked the two blocks to Holiday Inn and rode the elevators up and down. We got ice from the free ice machine and pretended we were guests at the hotel. We laughed and talked and just had girl fun."

Mother came home and Dad told her what I had done. She shook her head and left him to his job of getting the truth out of me. He kept me up most of the night and even when I went to bed I couldn't stay there for he came into my room and yanked me out of bed.

"I can't sleep, so you aren't going to either until you tell me the truth."

I held out for days, telling him the same story over and over, knowing he wouldn't believe me no matter how many times I told him. It never occurred to me to ask that he call Laura and find out if our stories matched.

Every morning the kids headed out to school and Mother left for work, leaving me to the tender mercies of my father. I felt like a worm stuck on a board with a needle in my spine, paralyzed by his fury, helpless to squirm out of it.

Finally, after the third day, I stopped caring about the truth. I just wanted the nightmare to end so I could go back to school and get out of my parents' bedroom. So I made up a story I thought my father would want to hear. I told him Laura and I went to her house and I had sex with her brother.

He put his head in his hands and wept like I'd just told him I had killed someone and received the death sentence for it. His disappointment flowed in rivers through wide-spread fingers, his nose dripped, and his eyes squeezed shut against the sorrow of what I had done.

As for me, I was just relieved to have it over. He would beat me now and forbid me to have anything else to do with Laura. But that would be it. I could get back to living.

But that's not what happened. If I had known the price of my "confession" I would have just kept sitting there on my Mother's bed until my head burst open or my heart stopped dead. By the time I knew, it was too late. The child who rode the elevator at Holiday Inn would die that night and a stranger would take her place. She looked like me and talked like me, but the essential element that made her really me fell into a deep dark well, drowned in my father's misery.

Just because we don't remember something, that doesn't mean we don't know it~

Chapter 28

When my mother came home that night, my father told her what I had done. For the second time that day I disappointed my parent, but this time it was my mother.

"Oh, Chelsey, how could you?" she said before walking out of the room.

Later that night, a relative called to say Grandma Betsy was in the hospital. Mother said she was going to go spend the night with her. *You're going to leave me here alone with him all night?* I wanted to say, but of course, I didn't dare say it. I begged her with my eyes not to go but Mother was never very good at reading what was in my heart by looking into my eyes. I think she was glad to get out of the house.

There is something about a man when he is plotting the betrayal of a child that is obvious to anyone who has endured betrayal. It is like a strange mixture of misery and excitement, tinged by self-pity. I sensed that "something" in my father and knew it was too late to run. A terrible thing was about to happen, and there was nothing I could do to stop it. He put the kids to bed that night with strict orders not to come out of their rooms. He made me go to his bed.

I said "he made me," but I still can't figure exactly how he did that. I don't remember him telling me to go to his bed, exactly, but I know that I had somehow got the message before mother left the house that I would not be spending the night alone in my bed. *All hope is lost, I am undone.* Like a prisoner led to the guillotine, I hung my head and swallowed my shame. I was smart enough to know, with my brain, what he planned to do, but I never expected to feel what I did. It shamed me, and it imprisoned me. It was like drinking arsenic in a glass of cold water—a glass held out to you by the person you once trusted, the person who dragged you into a hot, desolate desert and left you there to die. When he comes back and hands you that cold, clear, water, you will drink it down and pray that death comes quickly.

He kept me there until morning. I got up and got ready for school. I was half afraid he wouldn't let me go, but he did, with nothing more than a whispered warning, "If you tell anyone, Dad will go to jail." That warning discretely disappeared into the depths of my forgetfulness for almost twenty years. Just because we don't remember something, that doesn't mean we don't know it.

Memories are a strange phenomenon. They dart out and shout at you, and then they hide. They may come in the form of pictures, or feelings, or words. The exact contour of their shape and form is not to be trusted. They often belie their age. But their message is true and they are trying, the best they know how, to help us piece together the puzzle of our lives—not perfectly—but well enough to understand where we've been and how to go on from there.

That was my dad. Doing things to me, things I didn't understand—things that made me hate myself for feeling anything at all. Hate, regret, despair, and betrayal. Betrayed not only by my daddy, but by my own body as well.

Dad. Do fathers do what he had done to me the night before? I didn't think so, but then I didn't know much. I hoped I could be good enough to make sure it didn't happen again, but I had a sinking feeling deep down inside that an evil had been turned loose in the night and nothing I could do would put it back where it belonged.

• • •

There is nothing more frustrating than responsibility without power, and that was just the position I was given. We couldn't keep a caregiver because we were much too unruly for anyone to handle for long, so I was given the responsibility of caring for my five younger siblings after school and during the summers.

I tried to clean the house, an effort driven partly by my roach phobia. I knew those nasty little creatures couldn't harm me, but the thought of touching one of them or eating something one of them had touched sent my brain into a tailspin.

One day I had scrubbed the floor and waxed the hardwood on my hands and knees. I was so excited about how it looked and I couldn't wait to show Mother when she came home. Surely she would be proud of me when she saw what I had done.

Then the boys got in the house. One of them ate a banana and dropped the peel on my newly-waxed floor. The other stepped on it and squashed it into the shiny clean surface. I don't know if they were trying to be mean, but if they were I probably deserved it. I had, after all, locked them out in the heat of summer while I busied myself with cleaning in the comparatively cool house. But I didn't think about that then, I was so mad I yelled and the chase was on.

O'dell could always outrun me, but this time I was determined to catch him. Just as he reached the back porch, I grabbed at him, but instead accidentally knocked him off the edge where he fell the five feet or so to the hard ground at the bottom. Today's safety code would require a railing around a porch that high, but if there was one back then, it must have been one of the things on list from the city inspector.

O'dell was mad as heck. "I'm gonna tell Mother."

I knew I was in for it. Sure enough, when Mother came home, O'dell told on me and Mother came at me with fire in her eyes. I started to tell her that it was an accident and why I was chasing him, but she wasn't hearing it. I had hurt one of her children and she wasn't about to stand for it. She never noticed the shiny floors, or if she did she didn't say anything.

• • •

The roses were blooming on the chain-link fence in the backyard. I loved the deep red blossoms and picked a few of the flowers that came through our side of the fence. I wondered if anyone would put roses on my casket when I died . . . I closed my eyes to shut out the red-clay dirt and litter scattered around me, and watched my own funeral progress.

> There we were in the church. The family sat in the pews and cried while the organist played "Amazing Grace." The casket was a lovely silver with little brass rosettes on the side where

the poles for carrying went through it. The lid was up and there I was, my long, red hair fanned out all around me. I looked like I was asleep with one long-stemmed red rose held in my folded hands.

"She was so young," Aunt Julie whispered, standing with her arm wrapped around my mother's waist. Mother blew her nose, "She'll never know how much I loved her."

I pulled a rose off the rambling bush and felt a thorn prick my skin. "Ouch!" The pain brought me back to the present and I squeezed the blossoms in my hand liking the feel of the thorns against my palm.

• • •

They didn't call it cutting back then and it wasn't exactly the same because it left no scars. I didn't want scars so I scratched instead.

I never thought about it much until one day when I was in the seventh grade. I was scratching my head and digging into my scalp when I noticed a bunch of hair scattered around on my desk. My index finger felt wet and sticky. When I looked at it I was surprised to find it bloody.

I pulled my hair over the spot and hoped no one would notice. I felt the blood oozing out of my scalp onto my hair. No one said anything, so after a while I forgot about it.

The bell rung and I bent to pick up my books stashed under the desk. My hair fell forward and that's when it happened.

"Ooooouuu." The girl in the next seat to the right squealed. "You have a bald spot!"

Everyone turned and looked at me. I slung my hair back, hoping it covered over the spot and dashed out of the room. No one laughed. Most of my classmates were kind-hearted kids.

• • •

Sometimes it felt like my body was bursting at the seams with crawly creatures trying to get out and I reached as far around my stomach toward my back as my arms would go and curled my fingers into claws. I dug in just enough to raise welts, like the welts my father's belt used to leave on my butt and legs, and drug them across my body.

One day my sister, Suzanne, said, "Chelsey, you're going to have to stop doing that to yourself." I didn't think anyone had noticed. Another time, I drug a razor cross my wrist so lightly it barely broke the skin. I didn't dare kill myself and risk eternity in hell, so I tried to make my death wish known without actually accomplishing the deed. I worked at it for a while and got a sore on my wrist that scabbed over. Nobody noticed, which didn't surprise me much. I soon discovered other methods of escaping the misery of my circumstances—a ritual actually.

• • •

"Don't you want to lie down beside me and read for a while?" Dad said. The ruse had worked at first, but by now he might as well have spelled out what he wanted to do.

"I've got to finish the laundry." My voice sounded small, weak.

His silence told me he was pouting. That wouldn't have been so bad, but just as the lull before the storm is the eye of the hurricane, I knew him well enough to predict that his rage would soon flare out if I didn't do as he asked—except I wouldn't be the target. He would find a reason to bring out his belt and beat one of the boys, or pick a fight with mother when she got home. Sometimes he didn't have to pick it, she was pretty good at starting one up on her own. Either way, the end result was the same.

The worst part is that I never knew what was going to happen. What if one of the kids brought a friend home and Dad deliberately embarrassed them? A bad report card, a chore left undone, a disrespectful glance—anything could set him off and one of my siblings would pay the price for my resistance.

Maybe it would be like the time O'dell, who wanted to be a veterinarian, found a snake and brought it home. "I told you I wouldn't allow anymore animals around this place," Dad said, just before stomping its head off. I felt sorry for the poor little snake. He had died because of me. If I had done what I knew Dad wanted me to do before O'dell came home, the snake would still be alive.

"Dad . . . " I stood at the door, a laundry basket on my hip. "Would Uncle Bob do . . . you know . . . what you do to me . . . to Jeannie?"

The pained look on his face layered over the rage. "How could you ask me that, as if it was the same thing?"

"I'm sorry, Dad. I'm sorry. I guess I just don't understand."

I couldn't do it. I couldn't go in there one more time and participate in his little charade. So I didn't.

"I've got to go to the bathroom, Dad." I could almost see him smirk.

Then the ritual began. I'd look into the mirror and open my mouth as wide as I could. A scream with no sound poured out into the silence of the bathroom. After awhile I beat my fists against my temples. Sometimes I lay on the floor and curled my knees up to my chest, mouth clenched tight, muscles tensed. Hugging my arms close to my body, I pressed my insides outward, tensing every part of my body. Somehow, I thought I could make my heart explode if I pressed hard enough. It never did.

At some point it was as if my body, mind, and emotions were sufficiently numbed to get me through the ordeal waiting in my father's room. I took one final look in the mirror, fixed a smile on my face, and walked through the bathroom door.

What happened next is impossible to describe and if I could I don't think you'd want to hear it. It is enough to say that some body functions are governed by the autonomic nervous system, which operates without permission from the will of the person. Certain ways of touching trigger responses that betray the mind, will, and soul of a person and strips their dignity from them. They become a thing to be manipulated, rather than a person to be respected. Nothing a person says or does at that moment is coming from the part of them that makes a willful choice. Their will has been stolen from them and their body has become the plaything of a monster called abuse. Of course, I didn't know that then. All I knew was what I felt, and what I did, and of course I knew I had to make sure my secret never saw the light of day. No one can live with the humiliation of a thing like that.

• • •

I may have left my soul in the bathroom, but I took my imagination with me, right into the lair of the monster. Right up until the time that my autonomic nervous system took over and spilled his shame all over me, I imagined my mother would walk in to the room and see it all. She would run away from me and tell all her relatives what I had done so they could console her. Sometimes, I imagined my sisters or brothers came into the room. That was when I prayed to die.

It seems like the golden beam of light falling on that one ordinary thing, amid all the darkness, transforms it into the most glorious thing in all the world~

Chapter 29

All kinds of strange things started happening when I was thirteen. There seemed to be a secret agreement between Dad and Mother that I belonged to Daddy. Every time they got in an argument, Dad would tell me to "come on" and I'd obediently get in the car with him and ride around until he got ready to go home. We'd come in hours later, when mother was in bed asleep.

I won't say what happened on those long rides. I think you might already know, but it was horrible. The windows were down and wind poured through the car and sometimes light shone in and I was sure someone would see us. I hoped a policeman would pass by and figure out what was going on, but then I knew I'd die if he did because of what I was doing, too.

Then we'd go home and Dad would go back to being Dad, just as if nothing had happened and Mother would keep on being Mother, just as if nothing had ever happened. Sometimes Dad would take off with me saying, "We're going to the park," and I could almost hear the sigh of relief from Mother and the kids because they were going to get a break from Dad's chronic rage and unpredictable punishments. I don't blame the kids because they were just children and didn't have any say in the matter.

I learned a lot in the park. Every time we passed a parked car with a man and woman in it, Dad pointed out that the woman was probably another man's wife, since only cheaters went to the park to sit quietly in shaded arbors. Once when a couple walked down the wooded path hand in hand, he pointed out that they were probably having sex—see how she rubbed his arm with her free hand? Married people didn't do that unless they were married to someone else.

I learned that no one is to be trusted because everybody is cheating someone. I learned that the only way for my siblings and mother to get any peace was for me to go with Dad and console him because of all the hard luck and mistreatment he got.

At least I had some memories of when he loved me, before the night that changed everything. I remembered when we used to watch TV together and he put his arm around me. He was just being my Dad then, and cuddling me like I thought other fathers did with their daughters.

Then one day when we went to the park, he told me what he was thinking when he was lying beside me, watching TV. He told me what he went to the bathroom and did. I felt my stomach come up in my throat when he told me that. I didn't know much, but I was pretty sure most daddies didn't do what he did. He said it was because of something I made him feel and he couldn't help it.

∙ ∙ ∙

I don't want to paint a picture so dark that you can't see the dappling sun in it, because I've noticed that on the gloomiest of days there is often a stray sunbeam that settles on some small object, pointing it out to us. It seems like the golden beam of light falling on that one ordinary thing, amid all the darkness, transforms it into the most glorious thing in all the world.

That's the way it was with my baby brother, Willy. I loved holding him, feeding him his bottle, and even changing his diaper. That's how I came to thread one of those big diaper pins through his skin once. He didn't' cry much, so I didn't know what I had done until I changed him again. I felt horrible, but he giggled and cooed like it was nothing so I soon got over it.

Once I remember being really upset while I was taking care of Willy. He started screaming for his bottle, but when I gave it to him he pushed it away and kept screaming. I reheated his bottle, figuring that was the problem. Willy didn't like cold milk and I had been in such a hurry, maybe I'd just gotten it lukewarm. I heated the water in a pan and set in the glass bottle, which was the only kind we had in those days, all the while listening to Willy's screaming. I kept taking the bottle out and testing it on my wrist, just like Mother had showed. It seemed to take forever for the milk to warm up, and Willy's hollering never let up.

I lost it then. Something in me snapped, and I grabbed the bottle and ran into Mother's room where Willy was lying on a blanket on her bed. I threw the bottle against the wall above his head and yelled at him to shut up. The bottle broke into tiny pieces, falling in a crystal shower all round him. He screamed all the harder and I broke into sobs. I ran over and picked him up, scattering the clear glass on the floor and hurrying to the living room with him in my arms. He was mad but untouched.

I couldn't believe it when he stopped crying as soon as I picked him up and started walking with him. I cuddled him close to me and made my way around the house, holding him like that until he fell asleep. I guess babies need holding as much as they need feeding. Willy going to sleep cuddled against my shoulder was one of those stray sunbeams that lit up my day and gave me courage to face the night that was coming.

Chapter 30

I went to bed with my head pressed against the screen, trying to catch a breath of air in the heat-soaked house. The bedroom I shared with Suzanne and Dora was barely big enough for two beds, much less three, so Suzanne and I took turns doubling-up with Dora.

Dora, at three years old, brought out all my maternal instincts. She depended on me for just about everything, and I would have done anything for her. Her blue eyes brimmed with mischief, and sometimes with tears. I first discovered the wonders of a rocking chair when Dora was born. When she fell down and skinned her knee, I was there to pick her up and hold her. As she grew older, I would assume other maternal roles as well, but for now, I washed and dressed her, bragged on her and told her I loved her. Somehow I didn't realize until she told me years later, that the only comfort and nurture she got as a child came from me. Or maybe I did, because I would have died before I left her to the not-so-tender mercies of our parents.

That night Dora slept beside me, lost to the world. I couldn't sleep in the oppressing heat, so I thought I'd get up and wash my skin with cold water to cool down. I'd discovered that wet skin intensifies even the barest breeze, easing the heat-filled nights. The only problem was how to get across the hall to the bathroom without stepping on roaches.

Lots of houses in Arkansas had roaches, especially houses in the low-lying areas near creeks and rivers. We also had those big old water bugs that looked like a giant roach but could fly across the room. I was more scared of those things than rattlers and only slightly less afraid of common household roaches. I knew if I could just reach the light switch they would scatter back to their hiding places in the walls, so I'd squeeze my eyes shut and dash for the light, trying to get there before my brain had time to register the crunch of roach exoskeletons under my feet. Most of the time it wasn't worth the effort, so I'd just lay there staring up at the stars through the screen until morning cooled down the day just before dawn.

"Oh, God, please don't let them fight tonight," was my most frequent prayer. I dreaded the sound of my parent's angry voices and the crash of dishes or furniture that often punctuated Dad's sentences. The worst was when Mother would cry out and I'd know that he'd grabbed her arm and slung her into the wall even before I heard the thud. That's when I knew, I always knew, he would come to my bed. If I happened to be asleep he'd get mad at me, too.

"How could you go to sleep when you know what I'm going through?"

I didn't get the connection, but I always felt guilty for it, like a soldier going to sleep on guard duty or a night watchmen falling asleep on the job. Most of the time, I wasn't asleep. I just lay there wondering if he was going to kill her, and feeling guilty because I didn't offer to go for a ride with him so he wouldn't hurt her.

If only he didn't tell me to do the ugly thing that always came along with it, I might have actually enjoyed the ride. The night wind was a welcome relief blowing through the window like it did, and there was something soothing about knowing that mother and the kids were safely tucked in at home. It's just that the ride was never the only thing that happened. He talked on and on about what Mother did to him and how bad she was. Sometimes he talked about leaving and I hoped he meant it. I couldn't have told him that, because then he would have stayed and kept yelling and throwing things around. At the same time, I knew if he left I wouldn't have anybody to take my side when Mother was mad at me, which seemed to be all the time. At least he was kind some of the time, like when he doctored my sore feet.

All of us kids were barefoot more than we were in shoes. I often walked to the neighborhood grocery, oblivious to the hot asphalt on my bare feet. There were no signs stating "no shirt, no shoes, no service" in the grocery store back then. I ran around the yard in my bare feet, ignoring the broken glass, nails, and debris. So I was always getting something in my feet, and most of the time it set up infection. When the wound got red and ugly with little squiggly lines running from it, Dad would doctor me.

He'd get a deep pan of scalding water and pour Epsom salts into it. He'd tell me to put my foot into it slowly. I'd try, but the searing pain of the near-boiling water touching the inflamed wound caused me to draw back and started the tears flowing. That's when he'd take my foot in his left hand and use his right hand to splash the scalding water on my foot, gradually allowing my skin to acclimate to the heat. He'd always say, "See, I'm putting my own hand into it. If I can stand it, you can, too." I'd squeeze my eyes shut and bite down hard until the heat eased up. Then I'd look at the pan and watch the infection swirling out of my foot into the hot water. He said the salt drew it out. The relief was immediate. I don't know which felt the best, release from the pain in my foot or from the aching in my heart because, at least for the moment, Dad seemed to care about me.

How could my relief and deepest wounding come from the same person? I couldn't figure that out then, and I'm not sure about the answer now. I just know I loved the person who relieved my physical and emotional pain with an occasional show of tenderness. Even though he'd turn around and drain the life out of me with his unspoken but unmistakable demands. Somehow I learned to love my Dad and hate my abuser with equal intensity, a development that helped me survive, but also kept me locked into a nightmare from which I could not wake up.

• • •

Birthdays came and went as mile markers on my descent into hell. My body was growing older and my mind was growing up, but my emotions and ability to process them were locked into assumptions and understandings that I internalized right along with "you breathe air—not water," and "if you jump from the top of a tall building you are likely to die." Some things just were and there was nothing you could do about it.

THE GIRL AMONG THORNS

Life is made up of "if onlys" and "amens." The "amens" are the things we did that turned out right. The "if onlys" are the things that might have turned out right if only we had known something we didn't know, or had done something we didn't do. In my short life up to that point, "if onlys" far outnumbered the "amens."

So it is really important to remember the "amens." One of those amens happened when I was still thirteen. Grandma Betsy had moved to a project near First Assembly of God, where I went to church. They had a program for girls on Wednesday nights called "Missionettes." I loved the program. I didn't have any friends there, but at least the girls were nice to me, and I got to spend the night with Grandma after Missionettes and walk to school from there the next morning.

It gets dark really late in Arkansas in the summer, and I always walked the few blocks to Grandma's when Missionettes was over. One day I was walking along, trying to figure out what to do about what Dad was doing to me. It had started happening so often that it seemed like he was the abuser most of the time and my dad infrequently. I didn't think I could stand for it to happen one more time. I considered my options.

I could run away, but I couldn't take my siblings with me. What if I left and Dad started in on one of my sisters? Maybe I could go to a teacher or someone and tell them what he was doing to me and what he was making me do to him. *But he doesn't make me do it.* He just gets mad at Mother and the kids and takes it out on them when I don't do it and then gets over it when I do. *If I tell on him, I'll probably be in as much trouble as he is,* I thought. Then misery set in like never before, but I couldn't stop thinking about it because the problem was bigger than ever and I had to do something.

I had already tried talking to the only counselor I knew. Mrs. Brown was the Junior High Guidance counselor and one of the loveliest ladies I had ever seen. She was a head taller than most of my teachers and carried herself like the Statute of Liberty. When I closed my eyes I could almost see the torch in her hand.

The first time I sat across the desk from Mrs. Brown, I knew I had found a friend.

"What's going on, Chelsey?" she said, just as if she really knew me by name and not just as one of the students on her list of appointments.

How do you tell a pure stranger—even if she is a kind and lovely lady—the truth about something as dangerous as what was going on in my home? I wondered what Mrs. Brown would say if I just blurted it all out, told her everything. I wanted to, but I couldn't. I just couldn't bring myself to tell on Daddy, to risk making him really mad and then having to live with him after all. And what if they didn't believe me? What if they made me leave but left the other kids there—at Daddy's mercy?

I couldn't take that chance. So I said, "My Dad won't let me date." Pretty lame, I know. I was only thirteen. Lots of dads won't let their daughters date at thirteen.

Mrs. Brown looked at me with her solemn brown eyes, eyebrows raised. "Do you think your dad distrusts you?"

"Yeah."

"Have you ever given him reason to distrust you?"

"Yeah, I guess so." I was thinking about the time I sat by a boy on the bus coming back from singing with the ensemble, especially when I admitted I enjoyed it. And then I thought about the "song boy" and I liked that, too. I guessed maybe it was my fault after all.

I didn't give up right away. In fact, I went to see Mrs. Brown so often that some of my classmates started whispering when I was called to her office. I knew she meant well, but it just didn't do any good to talk about it. It was like I was talking about a whole different story than the one Mrs. Brown was hearing and I didn't know how to tell it any different.

So here I was walking to Grandma's on a Wednesday night, still trying to figure out what to do.

What if I ran away, I thought, *and didn't let myself think about what he'd do to my sisters and how he'd beat my brothers?* Then there was the problem of where I would go. I already knew that girls who ran away usually got raped, killed, or worse. The only thing I could think of that was worse was being forced into prostitution, and that wasn't a lot worse than what was already happening to me.

I could kill myself. That would take me out of the situation at home, but it would probably send me to hell, and that would be the same as option one because prostitution would do the same thing.

At that point, it hadn't occurred to me that I could kill him. That thought would come later, but it wouldn't just be a thought. It would be a very real possibility.

When I left the church, a light rain was falling. By the time I was halfway to Grandma's, it was raining in earnest. A car pulled up beside me and a middle-aged man reached over to swing the door open on the passenger side.

"Is everything all right?" he asked. I looked at him for a moment, trying to figure out if he was really concerned about me or just pretending. The crazy thought went through my head that maybe this stranger really did care if I was all right or not. If had believed that, I would have jumped into his car and probably never been seen again. But I didn't believe it. By that time I didn't think anyone cared very much about what happened to me, except maybe Grandma Betsy. So I shook my head and kept walking.

"Get in," the stranger ordered. That scared me. I moved over on the sidewalk as far as I could get and increased my speed. The stranger slammed his door shut and I heard him mutter, "Damn," as he drove away. That, I believe, was an "amen" moment.

Chapter 31

My brother, Mitch, could fix anything. He was always bringing home old lawn mowers and using the parts from one to fix up another. He had an entrepreneurial spirit that led him to start his own lawn mowing service. Mitch could talk almost anyone into giving him a job. He was pretty cute with his bright red hair and nickel-size freckles, but I think it was his slogan that got him hired. He made up his own business cards with his name and phone number on it and put his slogan at the bottom. It said, "A job worth doing is worth doing well."

Soon, Mitch had more lawns than he could mow, so he paid O'dell to take up some of the slack. It was going well until Dad shut his business down the second time Mitch set fire to his lawnmower. Mitch didn't take much care when he filled the gas tanks, so I'm guessing the combination of sparks coming off the mower blade hitting rocks and the hot Arkansas sun started the blaze. I was terrified that Mitch or O'dell would be blown to bits by an exploding gas tank, so I was secretly glad when Dad called it quits.

Mitch, whose creative mind never let him take no for an answer, decided if he couldn't mow yards he might as well fix up all the broken down lawn mowers he could find and sell them at a profit. It wasn't long before we had a lawn mower junkyard right in our backyard. The city inspector wasn't too happy about that, so Mitch got rid of most of the spare parts.

One day I was in the kitchen trying to outlast Dad's moping, a technique that sometimes worked. A phone call could get him out of the house or some kind of news, whether good or bad, could disrupt his mood, and I'd get a reprieve for a while.

I was putting something together for lunch when I heard O'dell screaming at the top of his lungs. I ran to the window and saw Mitch standing over him holding something metal in his hands. The other ends were hooked up to the lawn mower, which was running full bore. In between the two ends of the wires, O'dell was on the ground all wrapped up in the wires and flopping around like a gut-shot squirrel.

I tore out of the kitchen screaming, "Mitch! You're killin' him." By the time the door slammed behind me I was at the scene, bending over my prostrate brother, fully expecting him to be dead. He opened his eyes and looked up at me.

"I thought he'd killed me," he said.

"Naw," Mitch shook his head. "Lawn mower batteries won't kill anybody." He didn't even try to explain that he'd started out to pay O'dell back for all the times he'd given him a shock just for the fun of it, but the thing got out of hand when the lawnmower wouldn't shut off. Much later, I learned that he'd grabbed the wire to disconnect it and took the shock himself to save his little brother—but at the time I was mad enough to kill him.

I turned around and went back to the house, still angry, but trembling from relief. When the door slammed shut behind me, I heard Dad bellow from the bedroom. "What the heck do you think you're doing—screaming like that?"

I stomped into Dad's bedroom and stared at him laying there all sprawled out on the bed, and that is the moment I began to hate him. When he was pitiful, crying about how he couldn't help himself, I felt sorry for him and pity and love got all mixed up together. But when he was mean and selfish and mad, I wished he'd quit whining so much about wanting to die and just go ahead and do it.

I think it was the True Confession (magazines) that set me up for what happened next. It came, of all places, at church~

Chapter 32

Going small-game hunting was another splotch of sunlight. Hunting trips, which usually ended late evenings, included my father, Mitch and O'dell, and sometimes Grandpa Kelsey. I loved it when Grandpa came, because we usually camped with him. I sat close to him and looked up at the stars, felt the warmth of the campfire, and knew, in his own quiet way, he loved me.

Sundays after church we still went to the country every week, but things were starting to change. My cousins had discovered boys. Men actually, for most of their dates were with men considerably older than themselves. They started drifting in a different direction than me. I got more and more bound up with secrecy, and they got pregnant.

I wrote a song about them once and it was picked up by a local country-music band. It was called, "I Cheated My Baby When I Let Her Grow Up Too Soon." I took my guitar out to the country with me one day and sang it to Marcie. She said, "You wrote that for me and Darla, didn't you." I said, "Yes," and she put her arms around me and squeezed me to her chest. She was married at sixteen and moved away. Darla didn't bother to get married, or maybe no one proposed, because she kept having children, but didn't marry any of the fathers. I grieved for my cousins and their hardships in life.

The country lost its charm for me after the cousins drifted away. I didn't care for sitting around in the living room after dinner and listening to all the gossip. Everyone knew what everyone else was doing and no one was without an opinion. The most private details of less-favored family members were discussed behind their back.

I guess that's why my father began to hate Mother's family. He suspected she was talking about how he shoved her around and beat the boys.

It's not hard to win the sympathy of a child when you are the only person who shows that child any nurture or attention, even if the attention is questionable. But my dad took that to the extreme, like he did just about everything else.

He made up a ten-point list of what mother was doing to hurt him and make him so mean, and I was told to keep a journal of when and how she did it. Sometimes, she did the amazing feat of practicing just about everything on that list in one day. It took hours of walking around with Dad out in the park, giving him my undivided attention, to sort it all out and get it on record. Mother's folks had their place in assaulting my father's reputation, too, and he spent a good amount of time telling me how much they hurt him and how sad he was because no one could see how good and kind he really was.

Losing the respect of Mother's kin brought out the meanness in Dad. He kept going to the country every week right along with the rest of us, but he and Mother argued all the way home and kept it up for days.

Everywhere we went in the car, it somehow ended up that I sat in the middle between Mother and Dad and the rest of the kids sat in the back seat. Eventually we got a station wagon, but I still sat up front and the other kids scattered between the two back seats. I don't remember if Dad said, "I want you to sit between your mother and me," but I knew Mother wanted me there part of the time when she was mad at Dad. The rest of the time, she hated me being there. I never wanted to be there, but if I said so I could look forward to that horrible look of rejection and disappointment Dad kept for just that purpose. Worse, he might take me out on a ride just to get his hurt off his chest and I couldn't risk that.

Eventually, Grandma Kelsey zeroed in on me in after-dinner conversation, giving subtle hints that there was something wrong with me sitting in the front seat, taking my mother's place. Some remarks were made with a wink at other relatives, who seemed to know exactly what she was talking about. It was hard to hold my head up around my mother's family members after I sensed that they thought I was involved with my daddy in doing my mother wrong.

My intuitions proved right because Aunt Julie told me decades later that, "Mother always thought something was going on between you and your daddy."

I tasted bile in the back of my throat when she said that and, to my shame, tried to defend myself. She wasn't hearing it. Uncle Don may have been speaking for them both when he told my mother, "She wouldn't have stayed so long if she didn't want it."

It wouldn't have hurt so much if I'd had the good sense to consider the source.

I don't think Grandma Kelsey liked me much after I turned thirteen, and that made me sad because I remembered when she loved me a lot. She even took me, along with Suzy, to Oklahoma once to visit with her mother, my Great-Grandma Abby. Suzy and I lay in the backseat and stuck our feet out the window across from each other, liking the feel of the wind billowing through our dresses. We didn't even mind that Grandma's car didn't have any air conditioning.

I kept asking Grandma to sing my favorite song, and she sang it over and over all the way to Oklahoma. Actually, it wasn't my favorite song most of the time, just when Grandma was singing it. I knew she'd had a brother named Tommy who could have written that song because he started drinkin' and gamblin' just like the song said, and his mother, my Great-grandma Abby, mourned for him 'til the end of her days. I'd heard he went to prison for something he didn't even do and go himself killed before he could get out. I wondered if Grandma Kelsey was thinking about her brother and the heartache he caused her mother every time she sang that old song.

I loved hearing Grandma sing it in her country twang, but even more, I loved watching her sing it. Her face looked so earnest that I wanted to hug her every time she started it over. But I didn't.

Oklahoma had aged Grandma Abby, or maybe it was from the old Indian man she was married to, because she had new wrinkles that I didn't remember from when she ran the grocery store. She had a scar on her hand, too, that she got when she caught it in the wringer of her old washing machine. But I didn't notice any of those things right away, I just saw her smile—a big brown grin stained with snuff. Most people would have been amazed by the big hump Grandma Abby carried on her back, the result of falling in the snow with a load of logs in her arms when she was eight years old, but I was used to it and it never bothered me.

As soon as hugs were over, I followed my nose to the kitchen and stood there amazed. Tables had been brought in and filled with a feast like you wouldn't believe. All my favorites were there. Potato salad, fried chicken, homegrown tomatoes sliced in thick chunks, cucumbers bathed in vinegar, and best of all, strawberries soaked in their own syrup.

Right beside the strawberries was an angel food cake. I felt my mouth watering and gulped it down just in time, because Suzy'd come up behind me and she would never let me forget it if I drooled all over the food. Damn," she said. "Damn, damn, and damnation."

I looked at her like she'd lost her mind. Everybody knows saying those words will send you to hell. She grinned and grabbed a dipper full of strawberries, filling her mouth and swallowing without even chewing them.

"Come on," she ordered. "Mama said for us to set all this stuff out on the picnic tables in the backyard."

A cool breeze ruffled the oak leaves and plunked an acorn onto the wood table every so often. We got all the food transferred and I sat back in Grandma Abby's rocking chair and sniffed the mixed up smells of grilling hamburger, chicken, and hot dogs. There wasn't any steak on the grill, but I didn't miss it because I don't think at that time I even knew what it was.

All of Grandma's Indian husband's friends and family filled up the yard, laughing and carrying on. I just soaked it in and wished it'd never come to an end. Grandpa Caleb, as she told us to call him, looked just like a dried up prune with his crinkled skin and skinny arms folded over a plump belly. I might have liked him if he hadn't done what he did to Marcie when she was only nine. She didn't deserve it because she certainly didn't ask him to put his hands there. She might have never told if Uncle Terry hadn't jerked the blanket off her at just the right time to prove what Grandpa Caleb was doing. I hated Grandpa Caleb for that because Marcie was never the same. She took to crying a lot and got to be what Grandma Kelsey called "high strung."

I paid Grandpa Caleb no mind. I was looking at that big washtub filled with sweet strawberries. Suddenly, I focused in on it from across the table and saw movement in the tub. How could that be, when those strawberries had been sitting there for the past forty-five minutes without anyone touching them?

"Grandma!" I yelled, making everyone stop what they were doing and look at me. "There're ants in the strawberries."

I jumped to my feet and grabbed a dishtowel. I single handedly defeated an army of tiny red ants before they knew what hit 'em. Grandma was right behind me.

"Oh, no," she mourned. "We'll have to dump 'em all out."

I looked at all those dead ants floating on top and offered to do the dumping.

I'm ashamed to tell you what happened next, though you can probably guess. Before I do, let me say a word in my own defense. I dearly loved fruit and we only got it once a year, at Christmas time. Maybe an apple here or there, but never strawberries. We got blackberries occasionally in the summer when we picked them ourselves and ate them right off the bushes. We couldn't eat many of them even then because we packed them up in tin cans and sold them to our neighbors. So, I just couldn't stand to dump out all those delicious berries soaking in their own juice underneath that thick layer of dead ants.

I took the tub out to the back of the lot where I was told to dump them, and took a tablespoon out of my pocket. Feeling excited and a little bit wicked at the same time, I raked most of the dead ants off the top and dug in. Later, I didn't eat any fried chicken or potato salad because I was full of ripe red strawberries with a generous sprinkling of tiny red ants mixed in.

Grandma Kelsey noticed me looking a little queasy and sent me in to lie down. I fell fast asleep and by the time I woke up the dinner was over. I couldn't make myself feel sorry that I'd eaten half a tub of strawberries by myself, especially now that I felt better. I still remember the sweet taste of those berries and I've almost forgotten the gritty feel of the few remaining ants that I ingested along with them.

Soon after we returned from that trip, things started changing. We kept going to the country every weekend but I started getting out of there as quick as I could and visiting my Grandpa's brothers and their families who lived a block or two away.

I got acquainted with Aunt Marcie, who gave me "True Confession," magazines to read on the way home. I learned all about sex from those magazines and felt both guilty and a little excited when I read them. I think it was the true confessions that set me up for the next sorrow that came to me. It happened, of all places, at church.

• • •

I started noticing the bulge in men's pants. I didn't want to see it. I tried not to. I prayed that God would point my attention in another direction, but he didn't see fit to do that. Tight pants were in style about that time, and even men in suits seemed to like the fad. Now where do you go every week and just sit and stare for hours at a man who poses in front of you and represents God? When that man has a big package (that's what Suzy called a man's private parts) and wears pants that hang over it so that it shows it off, what's a girl to do? If I looked away everybody would know I was guilty as sin because I couldn't look at the preacher. If I looked at him, the only thing I could see was that big ol' bulge behind his zipper.

About that time, Suzy had started getting close to me. She came to our house often on her way to Aunt Julie's. She started letting me read her journal and it was explicit. I thought, she knows all about things like this, so I'll ask her what my inordinate attention to male anatomy means.

"Do you do that?" I asked.

"No," Suzy said. "That's just weird."

That made it worse than ever. Even Suzy thought I was weird for noticing men's private parts and she should know—after all, she had seen a lot of them.

• • •

The worst was yet to come. Not only did I sit in the front seat of the car between my parents, I sat on the outside of them, right next to my Dad at church. Half the time he'd reach over and take my hand and I'd hold it through the service. Part of me hated holding his hand. This was the hand that did things that made me want to die on a regular basis, but the other part of me thought that maybe he was just being a Dad now and my torn up heart ate up his love in spite of myself. Daddies are supposed to love their daughters, and part of me believed that when he wasn't in the "twilight zone," the man sitting beside me was my Dad. Just my Dad. I hoped he was holding my hand because he loved his daughter—not his "dirty little secret"—but his girl who just happened to be growing up.

Then it was Good Friday. The preacher invited everyone to come take communion with him and his wife. The whole family signed up. Then the most horrible thing I could imagine happened. Mother took the other kids and went to take communion, and Dad took me later. I was sick down to the tips of my toes thinking about standing there beside him just like I was his wife and not his daughter, taking communion from the preacher and his wife. I know my hands shook and my throat felt like it had a peach pit stuck in it. I'm glad I didn't have to say anything because I know I couldn't have squeezed one word out of my mouth.

The preacher handed my Dad the communion cup and his wife handed one to me, just like two regular old couples standing there celebrating the Lord's death. When the preacher started talking, I knew I was supposed to look at his face, to let him see inside my soul through the window of green eyes that went along with my red hair, but I just couldn't do it. I couldn't look him or his wife in the eyes. The only other place to look was down. And when I looked down, all I could see what his big ol' package stuck out there for all the world to see. My face turned red as my hair—I know because I felt the heat of it sizzling on my cheeks. The whole process couldn't have taken over a few minutes, but it lasted an eternity for me. After I drank the wine and ate the bread, I turned and almost ran down the aisle to get out the door.

I was so glad when that preacher and his wife moved on to shepherd other sheep. I hoped I'd never see them again and I think they hoped the same about me. They would have had to be a lot dumber than they were not to notice where I was looking that whole time.

I had a lot of other vices, too. In fact, about that time of my life I was overwhelmed with them. I hated the gossipmongers out in the country, but I had become one of them. I learned that nothing bonds you to someone like sharing a secret nobody else knows. I wanted, desperately, to bond to my mother, but I had no idea how to do it. I finally got my opportunity through her sister, Suzy. I sacrificed her without a second thought to get into my Mother's good graces.

Suzy had filled up her journal with writing about her sexual exploits. She read all the entries to me, stirring up both disgust and envy. She made the awful mistake of throwing her journal in our burn barrel. As soon as she left, I went and got it out.

I found Mother and said, "Mother, I'm really worried about Suzy. I think I should tell you what she has been doing."

So far so good. I had Mother's attention. I brought out the journal and showed it to her. Mother was aghast. She got so upset she called her mother up right away and told her about the journal. She covered for me, saying she found it in the burn barrel, a ruse which seemed to work. Success in evil endeavors usually sets us up for greater evil, which was the case with my gossiping. It would take a miracle to break me of the habit after being rewarded with such sweet success. Unfortunately, miracles sometimes come in the form of very unpleasant experiences.

After gossiping about Suzy with my Mother turned out so well, I began to perfect the art. I gossiped about Suzy to

Jeannie, and about Jeannie to Suzy. Then I passed along juicy tidbits about both of them to Mother.

One day Jeannie called me, a relatively new experience since my poorer relatives had just recently got phone service. She started talking about Suzy. Telling me what a low-life she was and how she was becoming a slut. I plunged right in, happy to make the connection. A few minutes into the conversation, when enough had been said to pin me irrevocably to the wall, Jeannie said, "Oh, Chelsey, did I tell you we are on a party line?"

"What do you mean?"

Suzy's voice came on the phone. "It means I just heard everything you said."

I screamed and threw the phone down. I ran into the bedroom and pulled my pillow over my head where I continued screaming into the pillow.

Mother came running. "What's the matter with you?" I told her between sobs and gulps of air.

She stomped into the living room and picked up the phone. For the first time that I could ever remember, my mother took up for me. She said words to her sister that I didn't know were in Mother's vocabulary.

What happened in the family stayed in the family and if someone broke the rule something terrible would happen to them~

Chapter 33

I think it was at about this time that Dad's cousin, Kendra, came to live with us. At first, I think I felt sorry for her. She had the sad misfortune of getting some kind of disease when she was younger that caused her bones to be shaped kind of odd. I'm not trying to be mean, but her face formation really did resemble that of Neanderthal man. She was broad in the shoulders as any man, and her hair was sparse and coarse. When she laughed it sounded like a tanker honking at the dock, and she walked like a gorilla. She seemed to think she had come to be my daddy's right-hand girl. She was going to go into real estate with him, so he spent a lot of time teaching her things. I don't think everything he taught her had to do with real estate. She was a willing learner.

Mother and Dad fought a lot more while Kendra was there. Mother stayed away most of the time and Dad and Kendra got real close.

One day they were boozing together, something Dad had just taken to doing, and they offered me some peach schnapps. I'd never tasted alcohol before, but I liked it. I liked the way it made me feel too, as if I didn't have a care in the world. It made me want to laugh. If I'd kept drinking and turned it into a habit, I think I would have been one of those happy drunks—certainly, not a mean one.

I remember, through my alcohol-induced fog, that mother came into the room and told my dad, "You shouldn't have given her that." Dad said something, I don't know what it was, and Kendra honked her loud crazy laugh. Then I said something that I'm still ashamed of today, considering I said it to my mother; considering also, that I said it on one of the few occasions when Mother was trying to protect me. I said, "Oh, why don't you just go take a walk."

In spite of the confused state of my mind, I still remember the expression on my mother's face. She turned around with disgust and walked out of the room. I went to bed and slept off the one and only intoxication I would ever experience. I had enjoyed it so much, and never got any bad effects from it afterward, that I figured it was a trap set by Satan himself to make me into a pathetic, life-long drunk, so I never touched another drop.

Dad, however, continued to drink with Kendra, and they found it necessary to take long drives together to discuss my poor mistreated dad. His depression was brought on, I suppose, by one or more of my mother's ten habitual abuses of my fine upstanding father.

A few months later, Kendra disappeared. No one knew where she went, or if they did, they weren't talking about it. Over a year later, she showed up back at her mother's house in Newport, Arkansas. She had found some way to get herself pregnant and brought her baby boy back with her. My mother counted back the months and figured that Kendra must have had a boyfriend hiding in the bushes somewhere when she lived with us in North Little Rock, because that is when the Neanderthal woman got pregnant.

• • •

It wasn't long after that when Mother went to live with Grandma and Grandpa Kelsey. I envied her. She could get away from Dad and leave the kids behind, but I couldn't do it. Somehow that didn't make sense to me, but I didn't think much of it. I knew what I had to do. But dad hated her for it.

"She's probably out there lying about me right now,' he'd say. "I ought to go out there and shut up her lying mouth."

Then he'd start in on Grandpa Kelsey. "Who does that old man think he is, harboring my wife like that?" I guess he thought her dad should have sent her home so he could make her behave just like he did the boys.

I could get mad at Mother, but no one could make me despise Grandpa Kelsey. My tall, thin Grandpa with the kind voice and gentle ways was everybody's friend.

Maybe that's why his teammates in the union made him their leader. Of course, that might have been because Grandpa was a hero. I once saw his medals from World War II and it made me proud. He never bragged about it. I wouldn't even have known it if my cousins hadn't found his old military trunk and got curious. I asked him about it once and he said, "We did what we had to do, Sis. They just passed out the medals to the ones who stayed alive."

I suspected he wasn't telling me the whole truth, but Grandpa didn't want to talk about it so I shut up.

Grandpa's face was tanned dark from spending every minute he could outside, and it had hardly any wrinkles. That was because there was a blow-up at the chemical plant where Grandpa worked and he, being the foreman and all, ran right into the middle of it to drag an employee to safety. The chemicals burned the top layer of skin off his face leaving it smooth as a baby's butt. I guess Grandpa was kind of my hero, too.

That's why it terrified me when Dad started loading his shotguns and rifles into the trunk of his Ford Fairlane, telling me he was going out to the country to shoot Grandpa.

"I'll show that old man who he's messing with," Dad said, throwing a blanket over the stash of guns. "I'm gonna kill the son of a gun."

I should have called the police. That would have ended all my trouble then and there. But the thought never occurred to me. Mitch told me later that he stayed awake in his room, waiting for Dad to return so he could find out if Grandpa was still alive, but it never came to him, either, that we could call the cops. You just didn't tell outsiders what went on in your home those days—at least we didn't. What happened in the family stayed in the family, and if someone broke the rule something terrible would happen to them. When you learn that early on, it becomes what they call a law, like the second law of thermodynamics, which says that everything will go from bad to worse. Those kinds of laws aren't meant for breaking.

The night was fully spent when Dad came back in the door. I half expected to see Mother walking along beside him, but she wasn't. He said Grandpa was real reasonable and told him he'd try to get mother to see the light. Mother came home the very next day.

• • •

I think Dad thought he'd been humiliated too much to be comfortable at Grandma's after that. He was always telling me how he could tell Mother's folks were talking about him, and I don't think he meant it in a good way. He started visiting Mother's cousin, Tommie, after that and taking his guitar down to pluck a few chords. When Tommie wasn't home he'd go in the house and wait with Tommie's wife, Carrie. Once I found the front door locked, but I didn't think much of it. I went back to playing with the kids outside until long after dark set in.

That's when I learned another lesson. Tommie's son, Jake, liked me a lot. He was about my age, but I didn't like him much. He had dirty fingernails and his breath always smelled like onions.

The cousins and I were playing hide-n-seek when I heard him come up behind me in the dark. Before I knew it, his hand was on my chest, resting just a few inches from my breast. I froze right there and felt his hand slip an inch lower. That's when I learned that even if you don't like the person you can still get powerful feelings from a hand resting there, not even moving and him not saying a word.

"Let's go in the woods," Jake whispered.

I broke and ran. When I tried the door it was unlocked and right after that Tommie came home and Dad picked up his guitar. He wanted me to sing some good ol' gospel songs, but I said I was sick and went back to Grandma's house.

I was glad when we didn't go to the country anymore. I'd had my fill of it.

Chapter 34

My favorite person was still Grandma Betsy. Unfortunately, she had come by the house one day when I was lying on Dad's bed, reading to him, and spoke her mind. She told my Mother, "Chelsey shouldn't be doing that. It just doesn't look right to me."

Mother didn't tell me what Grandma said, but she told Dad. It didn't keep Mother from sending me to Dad's bed, especially when they'd had an argument or Dad was upset, but it stopped me from having the privilege of going to Grandma's house. When Mother and the kids loaded into the car to go see Grandma, I was expected to stay home with Dad. I don't remember being told that exactly, but I knew. I don't think it was talked about, at least not to me; it just happened, like everything else that happened. I knew what to do, and I knew to do it without murmuring or complaining.

I was a bridge, spanning the gap between Daddy and everybody else. Like a bandage laid over a great big open gash, I laid down my life so everybody I loved wouldn't fall into a gaping hole and be lost forever. I don't mean to imply that what I did was noble, it's just that I knew my place and so, it seemed, did everybody else. To question or complain was to weaken the structure of the bridge.

Grandma Betsy didn't know that, so she questioned, not once, but three times, and Dad stopped going to see her. That wouldn't have been so bad for her, but Grandma had emphysema and was hooked up to an oxygen tank. She took a risk by speaking up, and accepted her punishment without complaint.

She called me one day, or at least, she called our house and I answered.

"Why doesn't your Daddy come to see me anymore?" She asked me.

"He doesn't go anywhere," I told her. "He stays right here in that bed and doesn't leave the house." Somehow, I thought that Grandma should understand that Daddy was the one to be pitied, he was sick and upset, and everybody out in "the country" gossiped about him. Nobody understood my Daddy, not even his own mother.

Grandma started crying. "I know that, Chelsey. That's why I'm so worried."

I had made my Grandma cry. My poor, sick, Grandma who never asked me why I didn't come see her anymore. I don't know what was said after that, but I know I hung up the phone feeling sad, and guilty, and responsible for everybody's suffering. I didn't think Grandma would want to talk to me after that, and I guess she didn't because I never heard another word about it.

• • •

Not being able to see Grandma set up a powerful ache in my chest, but even worse was staying at home alone with Dad while everyone else went to Grandma's. It was like there was a secret agreement between him and Mother that she could do as she pleased with the other kids as long as he could do as he pleased with me. When the kids came home chatting about what Grandma made for them to eat or something she said, I sat there all wrapped up in a secret silence that hid my sorrow and my shame.

When I was fifteen, Grandma died. That was when my tears dried up—at her funeral. I know I was there, but I don't remember a thing about it. Not one solitary thing.

• • •

About the same time, Uncle Harry got leukemia. Dad volunteered to drive to Newport every week and pick up him and Aunt Molly and bring them to Little Rock to get bone marrow transplants. He made it clear that I was to go with him. I tried, at first, to find reasons to stay home, but he made it so miserable on everyone that I stopped trying and accepted what I could not change. By now I hated every minute I spent with my father, and that was every minute that was not claimed by the school, which was the only relief I got.

One day Dad stopped at McDonalds to get us lunch. I went to the bathroom and returned to stand beside him in line. I felt a draft on the back of my legs. I started tugging on my full skirt, discovering to my horror that the hem was tucked into the top of my pantyhose. I calmly un-tucked it and smoothed it out then turned and walked over to sit down at a table. Never would I let my father know that I had done such an embarrassing thing. He would have accused me of deliberately mooning the entire McDonald's Saturday morning crowd.

While I was struggling to survive my father's sexual advances, my brothers were victims of his emotional and physical abuse. He once left so many bruises on Mitch that the school intervened. They called my Mother but she went down to the school and convinced them that Mitch, being a pale redhead, bruised easily and his condition was the result of responsible parental correction. What idiot would believe such a thing I still don't know, but she got my father off the hook. If she had told them his deeply held and often stated belief: "You might as well not whip 'em if you don't bring blood," Mitch's story might have had a different ending. He might have been saved years of pain and turmoil.

Meanwhile, Mother started letting Mitch and O'dell drive in secluded areas. Mitch was old enough to get his permit, but any misbehavior, no matter how petty, was reason enough to take away the privilege of driving. Once he learned to drive, Mitch decided to test his skills by running away and taking O'dell with him.

They stole a car and took off for Tex-Arkana. They might have gotten away with it, but Mitch was driving at speeds in excess of one hundred miles per hour and was clocked by a State Patrol Officer. The officer took off after him, sirens wailing, lights flashing, but Mitch didn't stop. He led the police on a chase that ended on the bridge over the Arkansas River that divides Arkansas from Texas. When the police officers saw that they had stopped a fourteen-year-old and a twelve-year-old, they were as shaken as the boys. They told us they had orders to shoot them on the bridge. They couldn't follow a car chase into the heart of Tex-Arkana, where innocent bystanders were almost sure to be killed.

The boys spent a couple of days in jail. I walked the floor and worried. I cried. I prayed. The boys knew they were in for a beating when they got home, as they certainly were. O'dell begged the police to keep him in jail to avoid the mutilation of his body and soul. But the police had met his dad, and they weren't buying it. Mr. Davenport had apologized for the crimes of his sons and assured them that he was, indeed, capable of rendering discipline to his wayward boys. There would be no mercy; the arm of the law sent my brothers home.

Our father waited their arrival in a silent rage and I felt like my heart was exploding with apprehension.

"They'll probably be sent to juvenile jail," my father said. "I don't know what to do with them, so it may be for the best." *The best?* Jail is never the best for a fourteen and twelve-year-old who are just trying to stay alive.

I'd heard about the way Mitch was treated in Tex-Arkana when he spent his first night in jail. Men twice his size threatened to beat him up, and that wasn't the worst of it. One of them got real friendly and he was scarier than the rest of them.

The boys' court date passed and they didn't go to jail. Then Dad started talking about putting the boys into a foster home. "I can't manage them," he said. "They need to go to someone who will knock some sense into them." Those words conjured up images of beatings with wooden bats and panicked me into betraying my fear.

"You can't send 'em away, Dad," I begged. After that he talked about foster homes a lot, telling me what happened to boys who were unfortunate enough to go there. I was certain the only thing keeping my brothers out of foster care was my timely intervention. I had to keep them out of Dad's way and defuse every volatile situation that threatened my father's fragile peace of mind.

• • •

Meanwhile, there were the trips to Newport. When my father dropped Aunt Molly and Uncle Harry off at their house and started home with me, my worst fears were confirmed. He pulled a little plastic packet out of his pocket and told me he'd picked it up back at the truck-stop. He told me lots of other things too, but I don't think you'd want to hear about them any more than I did. Somewhere in the middle of all that telling, he mentioned that he used to drive down that same road with my mother. I never could figure out why he wanted me to know that, but hearing it made me feel like my own mother's worst enemy.

It didn't bother him any. He acted like he thought he was a teenage boy who had just made a conquest. As he drove through the black night down a dirt road surrounded on both sides by cotton fields, he bragged about what he was going to do to me. My heart beat so hard in my chest that I thought it was going to tear itself out of me. My airways hurt and I could hardly breathe. I dug my fingernails into the palms of my hands and blotted every thought out of my mind. I've heard it's impossible to have a blank mind, but I know better. White noise on a TV screen took up the whole space of my mind. I know what he did, and what he made me do, but I don't know what I thought about it because my mind and my body were disconnected.

Pain, terror, shame, anger, disgust, sorrow. They were all there with me in the close confines of my father's car and they stayed right with me when I got home and marched into my bedroom. They settled down in my heart and took up permanent residence.

My mother was in bed asleep. She didn't even know some uninvited guests had come home with her oldest daughter, guests who refused to leave for a very long time.

• • •

My fifteenth year was the darkest year of my life. The day my father drove me down that dirt road out in the middle of nowhere and took the last shred of my dignity from me was the darkest day. Though the sun would rise in the morning, it would never rise in my heart with the same promise that it did before that awful day. I had become totally and completely one of the "bad girls" whom nobody wanted nor ever would.

Every life must have purpose in order to survive, and I resigned myself to mine. I was the chink in the dam of my father's rage, the object of his perversion. My only hope was to hold back the raging waters that threatened to wipe out the sole purpose I had left—I would shelter my siblings from as much harm as I could and do my best to help them have a normal life. In my heart and mind I became the surrogate parent to five younger children who thought I was my father's favorite and vacillated between needing me to plead their case and hating me for my exalted position—a position of influence over the man who ruled over us all by his rage and threats of violence.

My father, sensing his absolute control over me, offered me a way to accomplish my purpose with one fell blow. I could run away with him. We could get an apartment in Chicago or somewhere so no one would ever find us.

Terror colored every day as he tried to persuade me to do as he asked. One day he followed me around in the yard, harping on his obsession.

"I would miss Mother and the kids." I told him. My voice sounded as weak as I felt. My legs were trembling, and my heart seemed to have receded deep into my chest. I couldn't feel it pounding. I thought of what mother might do if he carried out his wish and took me away. She confirmed my worst fears when I asked her years later.

"I don't think there's anything I could have done," she said, just as if she was dropping hot tar on my head. "Your daddy always did what he wanted to do and there wasn't anything I could do to stop it."

Mother would have stopped it if it had been any of the other kids and we both knew it. That was the worst thing about it. I knew getting Dad out of there permanently was the best thing I could do for Mother and the kids, but I couldn't bring myself to do it.

• • •

One day when Dad was in his "twilight zone," which is what I call the space between when he started pressuring me to do what he wanted and when I finally gave in and got it over with, Dad grabbed my hand and moved his fingers in a circle motion against my palm and I felt like a dirty dishrag. That was the first time I felt the faintness come over me. It was as if my brain shut down but my body kept acting just like it always did. Compelling darkness swathed me like a warm blanket and offered sweet release. I didn't yield to it and it passed, but it would come again and then it would overpower me.

The faintness came again a few days later. I was in my room and I heard my parent's voices, loud and angry. Mother's voice was hard and patronizing, egging him on. *Does she want to make him madder?* I wondered. Sometimes it seemed like the two of them were creating a drama where they would fight over anything and everything just so Dad could take me off with him. He got what he wanted and Mother did too, a little time to live out her life without moving from one fearful moment to another.

Maybe that's why I pushed her off when she came running with a cold washcloth. I regained consciousness with her standing over me, looking all concerned. I said, "Don't touch me," in a voice that sounded like it came from someone else.

Mother reminded me of Sarah in the Bible who gave her slave girl to her husband and then hated her because he liked it. Except Sarah sent Hagar away and Mother didn't want me to go anywhere unless I took him with me. Who would get him out of the house so she and the kids could have some peace? We had a family system that worked as long as I did my part and pretended to want it. If my part broke down, everything would fall apart and the ones to pay the price would be the ones who least deserved it. I would keep the secret if it killed me, and I was pretty sure it would.

Every time I passed over the Arkansas River with its raging current and powerful undertows, I longed to throw myself into it and be done with it. Apparently, I wasn't the only one who saw the river as a welcome relief. I heard of others who jumped from the bridge and were pulled out by divers whose job was to disentangle their broken bodies from the debris at the bottom of the river.

I could kill him, I thought, then I'd never have to do this again~

Chapter 35

I never knew when I would be awakened from sound sleep by my father shaking my shoulder, telling me we had to go now. My chronic fatigue made it difficult to concentrate in school and weakened my immune system. I started coughing, harsh hacking coughs that practically took my breath away. After a while I was coughing up blood. Test results showed I had something called "Arkansas Fungus" on my lungs. There are three scars on my lungs to this day because of the coughing disease. When I kept coughing up blood, they finally decided to take me to the doctor. I think they thought I was going to die, because Mother took me to K-mart and bought me three new dresses. It was like the last meal before a hanging. You can spare a little time and money on someone if you know it's the end.

I stayed alive and Mother and Dad kept entertaining the neighbors with their fighting. The arguments were fiercest over who was the best real estate salesperson. Dad claimed Mother "stole his glory." He said he worked up the sale and then everyone in the office gave the credit to Mother. I didn't see how he could have worked up much of anything when he spent most of his time at home making life miserable for us.

It was during this time that Dad's life was in danger, though he didn't know it. Dad took me and the boys—all except little Willy—small-game hunting. My love for the woods was one of those splashes of sunlight on the dark canvas of my life. We all spread out in different directions. I found a spring-fed pool at the bottom of a deep ravine. The clear water reflected the deep blue sky above, giving it the appearance of an aqua bowl. Oak trees that reached upwards of sixty feet spread their branches over it and dropped acorns on its smooth surface. I rolled up my pants and took off my boots so I could rest my feet on the rocky bottom about two feet down. The birds gossiped overhead and a slight breeze swept through the oversized leaves of summer. I leaned back against the nearest tree and closed my eyes, breathing in the fragrance of the earth and sky.

Then I heard the crunch of twigs under booted feet. I bolted upright, alert for armed hunters who might mistake me for game. It was a hunter all right. It was my father and he was hunting me.

"Come hunt with me," he said.

It wasn't the first time he had found me in the woods, so I knew what he wanted. I followed a few feet behind him, a battle raging in my head.

I could kill him, I thought, *then I'd never have to do this again.*

No, another part of me resisted. *I can't kill him. He's my dad.*

No. Fathers don't do what he does to you.

But I let him do it. I don't make him stop.

Yeah, and you know what will happen if you don't let him do it—and act like you want him to at that.

If I kill him, I'll go to prison, or the insane asylum.

It would be worth it.

What if I just wound him and he kills me instead?

Then I would visualize him lying on the ground, shot in the head, bleeding all over the leaves and on my feet. I killed my abuser, but my Dad is lying on the ground crying because I'm his daughter and I killed him, too.

My head hurts. I can't think any more.

Dad stopped walking and waited. I can't tell you what he did because it is a shame even to speak of things that are done in darkness, according to the Good Book. I wished I had shot him. Someday, I decided, I probably would.

Dad looked at his compass and pointed north. "This way to camp," he said, cheerful as can be. I couldn't get that. He had just destroyed my life and he was smiling like he won the Olympics. That's when he fell down the ravine. I ran after him. I had just tried to make up my mind to kill him and now here I was chasing down a ravine after him to make sure he hadn't hurt himself. His ear was bleeding from where it got caught on a tree branch. He didn't bother to wipe away the blood, but wore it proudly into camp. Mitch saw him come up with blood running down his neck and me right behind him. He glared at me, "What did you do to Dad?"

There I had it. If I killed him I could expect no sympathy, even from my brother who got the beating of his life every few weeks. Dad griped at Mitch all the way home, but I can't for the life of me remember what it was about.

• • •

I don't know if you'd call what I did fantasizing, but I did it a lot. It came on me without any warning and left when it was ready. All kinds of things happened to me, to my siblings and to my mother that made me mad, made me grieve, and sometimes gave me joy, things that happened entirely in my mind.

In my mind, Dad decided he had enough of all of us and took off for Alaska. His boat sank on the way there and we all grieved, just like people are supposed to do. Part of me really did grieve—the part that still believed a little bit of daddy was left inside the monster who had consumed most of him. The rest of me was happy that he was gone and I didn't have to go with him on any more rides.

Sometimes, I dreamed up things that made me want to hide myself. I wondered if those dreams were a part of me or some kind of aura spinning off the monster who lived in our house. Someone asked me once if I'd ever had a thought of doing something terrible to anyone else. I had lots of thoughts of doing terrible things to Dad, but never to mother or my siblings. I had thoughts about people taking off their clothes and standing naked in front of me, but I didn't enjoy those thoughts. They came without my consent and left when they pleased.

It seems to me that people have two kinds of thoughts. Some of them come from your wants, like my want to get rid of the monster who hurt my loved ones and would have hurt them worse if I hadn't done what Dad wanted me to. Those kinds of thoughts come from my heart, I think, because they line up with my wants. Other kinds of thoughts come from my hurts, thoughts like seeing people naked when I don't want to see it and I take no pleasure in it. Those kinds of thoughts aren't my thoughts—they belong to the hurts inside me and when the hurt goes away, they will go away too.

Chapter 36

Mitch didn't want to kill his Dad, but he tried to kill our brother O'dell. I don't think he really wanted to kill him—it's just that O'dell was gifted at doing things to make people really mad and then outrunning them. When Mitch figured out that he'd never be able to catch up with O'dell, he got out the twelve-gauge shotgun and shot through the bedroom window. Since it didn't have any glass in it, I guess he figured he wasn't damaging anything.

O'dell ducked into the storage shed at the back of the lot. A neighbor finally told our dad because he didn't want O'dell's blood on his hands. Dad didn't believe it until he found the side of the shed full of shotgun pellets.

Mitch wasn't the only one who was mad enough to shoot O'dell. I never attempted it, but I won't say it didn't cross my mind. Especially when I went to a whole lot of trouble to make fudge for the kids, a rare treat, and O'dell found a way to break into the house through the bathroom window and steal the fudge. I caught him once and nearly grabbed hold of him. Slippery as a fresh caught fish, he slipped out of my grasp and ran for it. I chased him. The girl who never swore broke her own rules. I'm ashamed to admit it, but I came out with a good profanity or two, and then realized Doc Holiday next door was watching me and listening. O'dell registered the good doc's amazement and doubled over with laughter. I wasn't mad any more after that. I went home worrying about my eternal salvation and wondering if "hellfire and damnation" was enough to lock me out of the pearly gates forever.

• • •

O'dell, like me, stayed alive by living largely in his imagination. His imagination got him into all kinds of trouble in the seventh grade when he made up an extraterrestrial friend named Genko. No one bothered him about Genko until one day in junior high school when he beat up a classmate because the kid took a seat beside him, a seat already occupied by Genko. He had warned the kid not to sit there, that his green-skinned friend from another planet was already occupying that spot. The kid laughed at him and, much to his regret, sat there anyway.

"I hit him before I thought about it," O'dell said in his own defense. "What would you do if someone sat on your friend and he couldn't protect himself? Any self-respecting person would take care of it for him."

It made sense to me, but the principal had no appreciation for imagination so he suspended O'dell for three days. O'dell had a hard time sitting down when he went back to school, but he kept his green-skinned friend to himself thereafter.

Due to all the trouble my brother had experienced in his young life, he turned his room into the kind of sanctuary you might expect of him. His dresser became his practice board for a switchblade knife. He learned to get that thing open and hit a speck on his dresser with it before you could say hello. His other accomplishment was the fermenting of grape juice to produce his own red wine under his bed. I respected O'dell's creativity, though our father was not quite as tolerant.

• • •

Mitch had a different way of handling things. While O'dell made a practice of hitting people, Mitch was always getting himself hit. He nearly got us both murdered when he was in Junior High School and I was a freshman in High school.

First off, Mitch didn't know a thing about diplomacy. He was likely to say the first thing that came to his mind, which might have been all right if we'd lived in a better neighborhood, but boys in our neighborhood would just as soon fight as spit.

He never learned his lesson about borrowing money he couldn't pay back, either. The money Dad gave Mitch for lunch was inadequate, so there he was in the cafeteria every day of the week, except weekends, smelling all those good food smells and too broke to buy any of it. He always spent his week's lunch allowance the first day— he just couldn't help it. He was in the process of shooting up from the short stocky body of a child to a height that would keep him out of the Air Force in later years. But that would take awhile. He was still a stocky, freckled-faced, redheaded boy when he got tangled up with a group of students who were bussed into the all white school against their will.

One day, one of those students who had been gracious enough to loan Mitch a lunch token demanded repayment. Mitch had only enough money for a sandwich for himself and he was starving. When he refused to turn over his money, he found himself surrounded by the lender's friends. They all agreed he should surrender his coins. Mitch, being the bright kid that he was, threw the coins on the floor.

"Fine," he said. "You want it, you pick it up." He turned and stalked away, but not before he heard four of them plotting his final destination. They would catch him after school and make him pay for his disrespect.

That's how Mitch happened to show up on the top step of Ole Main High School the minute the bell rang. He had cut class early and ran all the way to my school so I could walk home with him. When I came out and he told me his story, I asked if the boys had followed him.

"Square and Tom did," he said. He pointed to a short, stocky black boy who obviously hadn't got his growth spurt either.

"Oh. We can take care of him," I said and started down the steps, my arms full of books.

"Uh, Chelsey . . ."

I turned impatiently and stared into the leering face of the tallest boy I had ever seen. Sweat glistened off his ebony skin and he carried a chain in his hands that looked like it came off a tractor hitch. I almost dropped my books.

"That's Tom."

"He's in junior high?" I asked Mitch.

"Got held back a few years," Mitch said without taking his eyes off the boy who just stood there, slapping the chain against his palm.

"Wait a minute," I told Mitch, glad for the protection of the schoolyard with its teachers and guards. "I'm gonna go talk to the principal."

Just then I looked down at the street about thirty steps away and saw our Dad pull up in his Ford Fairlane. It was the first in a long time that I had been glad to see him. Mitch and I dashed to the car and began telling our father the whole story.

At some point Dad noticed that Mitch was carrying a tennis racquet. "Where'd you get that?"

"Coach gave it to me," Mitch muttered without looking up.

"Where do those boys hang out after school?" Dad asked, his lips thinning out in a pale gash across his face.

Mitch gave him an answer, but he had learned his lessons before and knew better than to tell him the truth. Dad whirled the car around and took off to catch up with the black boys threatening his son.

"This it?" He pulled into the parking lot Mitch had indicated.

"Yeah."

"Gimme that tennis raquet." He took it from Mitch. "No white boy ought to need a tennis racquet to take four niggers," he said.

I hated it when Dad referred to black people like that. If they were what he called them, then we were poor white trash. I had no illusions at this point about the poverty of my family. There had been too many visits from housing inspectors who insisted that they were going to fine us if we didn't clean up our yard and put the window panes back in our house. We were blight on an already blighted neighborhood.

Mitch didn't say a word, just opened the door and got out of the car, his face white as death. Dad drove off, leaving him standing alone in the middle of that broken-up asphalt lot. When the bullies didn't show, Dad figured he had been right. Four tough black boys from the North Little Rock projects were scared to tackle his short, freckled-faced boy with the red hair and white skin.

Mitch knew better but he wasn't telling. He was just glad to be alive.

Chapter 37

It had been a long day with Dad and Mother arguing and trading insults, acting like they hated it but both of them enjoying it. Mother went on off to the real estate office and Dad told me to sit down and talk to him. He was drinking a beer, something he had taken to just lately. He had a bunch of pill bottles setting on the table in front of him, and he started opening them, glancing at me every once in a while to make sure I was noticing. Then he started talking about how mixing pills with alcohol can kill a person. Before I knew it he swept the whole pile of pills into his hand and downed them with a swig of beer. He washed them down with another beer, and then realized he had drunk the last beer in the house.

"Come with me, Sis," he said. I hoped he had gotten over wanting to die, because while I didn't especially want to live, it would be the final humiliation to die in the car alone with him.

That's why I begged him to quit when he aimed the car at a telephone pole and stepped on the gas, swerving just before impact. After two or three times of playing his game, I just shut up. Begging Dad not to do something was like egging him on. I thought I'd never live to make it home, but I did. I wanted to tell Mother what he'd done, but I never said a word. Why give them something else to fight about when it wouldn't change a thing?

• • •

Going to school gave me a daily reprieve from the constant bickering and Dad's chronic demands. That's why I felt like my life was coming to an end when I quit school in the tenth grade. I had been struggling all year with the coughing disease that scarred up my lungs, but I hadn't missed school because of that. I had missed a lot of school because I was expected to stay home and keep the peace between my two angry parents.

One day I went to school knowing things might get violent at home. I worried myself sick. I went to the school nurse and asked to go home. I didn't have a fever so she said no. I asked to talk to the school counselor, Mrs. Dean, who didn't remind me the least bit of Mrs. Brown.

"I need to go home," I told her.

"You don't have a fever, Chelsey," she said. "Why should I let you go home?"

"I don't feel well."

Mrs. Dean raised her eyebrows. "You don't feel well."

I shook my head. "I've got to go home." I insisted.

"Just sit in the nurse's office for a while and see if you don't feel better," Mrs. Dean said.

I sat there with my mind going crazy. I kept thinking of all the things my dad might be doing to hurt my mother, and then I'd think about her sharp tongue and get mad at her for provoking him. Then I'd think about him pushing her around like he sometimes did and I'd feel sorry for her. Worst of all, she'd started talking about leaving again lately, and I hated her for that.

Mrs. Dean came back in the room, a patronizing smile on her face. "Your father is on the way to get you," she said. "Your mother called and told me some things that I didn't know about your family. So go on. You may wait at the door until your Dad pulls up."

I wondered if I looked terrified as I considered these words. What had my mother told Mrs. Dean? I picked up my books and left the room with my eyes staring at the floor. Dad arrived a few minutes later and my feet dragged as I walked to the car. Sure enough, Mother left. Dad said she was going to Michigan to stay with her brother for awhile. At least she was out of harm's way. I knew the same wasn't true for me.

Later that day mother called. She said she wanted me to talk to Dad. He wouldn't come to the phone.

"Tell him I'm at the Arkansas River," she said. "I'm going to jump."

I told him.

"Tell her to jump," he said.

I told her. "He said jump."

"Fine then. I'll jump!"

The sound of my heart pumping blood roared in my ears when she said that. I wondered how I could hate her enough to want her to do it and love her enough to hate myself for wanting it at the same time. The thought of mother falling through the sky from the high bridge that spanned the river between the twin cities of Little Rock and North Little Rock took over my brain then and I would have jumped for her if I could. I imagined her hitting the water with a gigantic splash and disappearing beneath the mighty current of the Arkansas River. The room began spinning in circles and closing in on me. I've been told I started screaming at Mother and telling her to go ahead and jump.

Somehow I got it through my brain that she wasn't jumping after all and I started begging her to come home. I promised her that if she did I would quit school and work with her and Dad so things would get better. She must have believed it because she came back and I quit school.

It was easier said than done. I had to go to every teacher and tell them that I was quitting. Some of them just signed the paper releasing me from their class, but others tried to tell me that I was making a mistake. How could they know the pain that pounded through every cell in my body as I signed away my last bit of freedom and consigned myself to a fate worse than death? Didn't anybody see the agony etched in my eyes? If anyone had bothered to look at me, really look at me, they would have seen a tortured child as lost as a needle in a thorn bush. Maybe that's why no one took the time to look—it can be painful retrieving a needle from a thorn bush.

Chapter 38

I figured if I was going to be of any use to my parents in their real estate business, I ought to get some business training. I was the youngest student at Olivet School of Business in Little Rock, Arkansas. I made straight A's. I enjoyed every class except marketing. Mr. Knowles, the fiftyish teacher with big brass-rimmed glasses liked rubbing my arm as he talked. He was a foot taller than me and had a slight protruding belly, so he always bent his head to get closer when he talked to me. His breath smelled like fresh Listerine and I wondered what else he did to get ready to talk to me at the start of class. That's the only class I made an A- in, and I wouldn't have got the minus if I hadn't waited until the bell rang every day to make it into his class.

• • •

For awhile it looked like the sacrifice of my education would not be in vain. Mother and Dad fought less and I did my best to smooth out the rough spots, taking over the family budget and balancing the checkbook. I soon learned that keeping the peace had little to do with a balanced budget and a whole lot to do with providing my father with more access to me. Staying out of his way became increasingly difficult. By the end of the summer, I insisted on returning to school in spite of his threats, tantrums, and ever increasing despair.

When school started in the fall, I was one of the first students in the door. I started planning for college from the start of my second attempt at tenth grade. When SAT testing came around I received a certificate for scoring in the top 97% of my class. Considering my history and my continued poor grades, I think my teachers thought I had cheated on the test. They didn't realize that reading was my escape—a survival mechanism that I thoroughly indulged or they might have believed I really earned my scores.

Chapter 39

I was thrilled when I finally got my driver's license. I knew my siblings needed something to pour themselves into that would help them think of others more than themselves. Now, at eighteen years old, I could provide the transportation. So I got the idea of taking them to homes for the elderly. I called nursing homes and asked if we could come and sing for the residents. We were welcomed with open arms. I played the guitar, Mitch played bass, O'dell was on the drums, and Suzanne and Dora sang along with me. The boys backed us up singing, too. We always brought boxes of cookies and the home provided lemonade. Our audience was enthusiastic and ever so grateful. We went home feeling proud of ourselves and full of accomplishment. We had reached out and touched the lives of the less fortunate and they had rewarded us with smiles, hugs, and oodles of compliments.

Great-Grandma Abby took sick and had to be put in a nursing home. Grandpa Caleb had died the year before, and though I am ashamed to say it, I bid him good riddance.

I loved Grandma Abby and went to see her as much as I could. I got the kids in to sing for her at the nursing home, but one night she was too sick to come down and join the others in the meeting room. When the meeting was over, I took my guitar up to her room. I tiptoed close to her bed and found her sleeping.

I don't know how many times I had sung "Amazing Grace" for Great-Grandma Abby, but she loved to hear me sing it. So I did. I sat on the chair by her bed and strummed the guitar, singing to Grandma Abby for the last time. When the song ended, I held her hand and told her I loved her. The next morning Grandma left this world for a better one. I was glad I'd said good-bye.

• • •

All of us kids loved fishing. Dad and I, Mitch, and O'dell had fished often on the Burns Park Bayou off the main stem of the Arkansas River. One night we were floating along with the current when a catfish almost as long as our twelve-foot boat swam past, his slick body illuminated by the amber glow of our lantern. That's when Dad started talking about getting a real fishing boat, one big enough to take out on the river. Mitch and O'dell had saved a few dollars and they offered to throw in their part if Dad would buy us a fiberglass boat. What they didn't have they'd work for until their part was paid off. Dad took them up on it and before we knew it we had a sixteen-foot fiberglass boat with a sixty-five horse-power Evinrude motor sitting in our yard. We decided to take it out the first day and give it a try on the Arkansas River.

When we got to the boat launch we were in for a surprise. There were people everywhere, along with police cars, ambulances, and park rangers. While Dad pulled the boat out of the way, the boys and I got out and joined the crowd at the river's edge. That's when I saw the cadaver. The paramedic took the gurney right past us on the way to the ambulance so I got a real good look close up.

The deceased was a young male, about twenty-five. His skin was a whitish color like the thin piece of skin on top of a blister, and his lips had turned blue. But it was his arms that startled me. They were frozen in a swimming posture as if he had kept on swimming right up till rigor mortis set in. Suddenly, I felt sick to my stomach. I wanted to go home. The boys looked as sick as I felt. Besides, it was getting late and darkness was closing in. The last thing I wanted to do was launch out into that black water now that the sun had set.

A stiff breeze kicked up just as the gurney slid into the ambulance and the people began to clear out around the boat ramp. As soon as the ambulance pulled away, Dad backed our beautiful turquoise Sea-Ray into the water. We were going and there was nothing to be done about it.

The next week we took Suzanne and Dora along and then Mother and little Willy joined us. Sometimes I almost believed we were a normal American family out for a picnic. Dad always behaved when we were out on the boat because we were never alone then. I loved the boat and I adored the river, until one day when Dad decided we should set a trotline across the Arkansas River.

A trotline is a piece of strong nylon that has vertical loops with hooks on the ends strung along it. The idea is for hungry fish that pass up and down the river to take the bait and get caught on the hook. Then the fisherman "runs the line" by pulling the weighted line up a little bit at a time. The excitement starts when you put your hands on the trotline and feel it jerking against your fingers. That's when you know you have a fish on the line and you can't wait to get to it and haul it in so you can see how big it is.

In order to get a trotline across the river you'd have to tie it to a tree on both sides of the river and weigh it down as you move along so boats that come over the river won't cut the line with their propellers. I wouldn't have worried about the project so much if we had started earlier in the day, but we got on the river near nightfall with the whole family on board.

Mother sat in the middle with Willy in her lap and the rest of us took our places. Dad sat at the front and tied on loops with a hook at the end. Mitch was next, adding more loops and hooks, and I was after him, doing the same. At the back of the boat, O'dell held the line to keep the boat straight and tried to stay awake. A chill breeze sprung up and my teeth began chattering. The other kids looked cold but no one was complaining. Suzanne and Dora held flashlights, shining them on our hands as we hung the hooks on the line, and Mother held the kerosene lantern next to her and Willy.

All the while Dad kept reminding us of that monster blue-catfish we were going to catch. Blue Cat were ten times better eating than the old mud cats we caught on the bottom of the bayou. After a while none of us cared about the blue-catfish, we just wanted to go home.

Dad was afraid the line wouldn't go all the way down with regular sinkers, so he disassembled the steps to our storage shed so he could weight the line with half a dozen concrete blocks. By the time the blocks had been tied out along the way and sunk beneath the black surface of the water, it was becoming very difficult to hold on to the line. We were holding the weight of the blocks, the boat, and all its occupants against the drag of the current.

Then the unthinkable happened. The line snapped. I saw the white flash of nylon twine shoot into the air, and then I felt the slide of the line between my fingers. I thought of all those hooks Dad, Mitch, and I had tied onto the line, and remembered that O'dell was right in line to get hooked by every one of them. I pictured him wrapped in barbed hooks and twine, sinking beneath the water's surface, drawn to the depths of the Arkansas River by the concrete blocks Dad had tied onto the line. Instantly, I squeezed my hands around the line. If my brother was going over, I was going with him. I felt the line slice into my fingers, saw blood spurt onto my clothes. I turned to O'dell and ran my fingers over his chest where hooks had torn into his clothing. Not a single hook had lodged in his skin. The blood smeared over the front of his shirt was from my hands.

That was the last time we were foolish enough to span the Arkansas River with a trotline, but it wasn't the last time we would face death on the river. The next time, tragedy was almost certain to catch up with us.

I agreed, wondering what kind of pain Ms. Rita was in that would make it better for her to be dead~

Chapter 40

While O'dell's first love had been Donald, Dora's was Grumpy, the soft gray kitten that picked her for his favorite. He'd hiss, bite, and growl at just about anybody else, but Dora couldn't do anything wrong as far as Grumpy was concerned.

One day the boys discovered that Grumpy had an amazing talent. He always landed on all four feet—right side up. Every time you dropped him, from any height, Grumpy performed a perfect landing. They decided to test his skill by climbing on top of the swingless a-frame in our backyard and dropping Grumpy off it. Sure enough, Grumpy landed soundlessly on all four feet.

Dora stood back watching, uncertain about the game the boys were playing, but thinking it must be okay because you can't really get hurt if you land on your feet, can you? By nightfall, Grumpy was obviously hurt. He was very, very, sick. He didn't touch his food or water but curled into a little ball and refused to move. By morning, Grumpy was dead.

Mitch and O'dell were just as surprised as Dora that Grumpy died. But no one grieved more than she did. O'dell proved his sympathy by digging a grave in the backyard for Grumpy and Mitch made a tombstone out of two pieces of wood tied together in the shape of a cross with the words written horizontally: HERE LIES GRUMPY OUR BELOVED CAT.

We never got another cat, which was strange considering the abundance of cats that roamed our neighborhood. I think our near neighbor, Ms. Gloria Spline and her spinster sister, Rita, were responsible for that.

I thought Ms. Gloria was ancient, all wrapped up in her fine clothes and flashy jewelry. The soft folds of her pearl white skin wrapped themselves around gobs of makeup, which must have taken hours to apply every day. She liked bright red lipstick that made her look like her lips were bleeding, but her eyes were kind. Maybe she was too kind, considering what happened to her.

Her sister, Ms. Rita, was the exact opposite of Ms. Gloria. She stayed home and minded the cats while Ms. Gloria went to work every day at Mr. Hill's neighborhood pharmacy. Ms. Rita wore a print housedress every time I saw her and no makeup. She was practically invisible next to Ms. Gloria, but I think she liked it that way.

Everyone in the neighborhood knew that Ms. Gloria and Ms. Rita kept dozens of cats in their house. You hardly ever saw the cats outside. I thought maybe the sisters were afraid they would run away or get killed on Park Avenue, so they kept them in the house all day.

You'd think, with her being home all day like she was that Ms. Rita would clean up after all those cats, but she never did. People called the sister's house "the cat house" because it smelled up the whole neighborhood with the odor of feline bowel movements.

One day some of their mail got delivered to our house, and I was assigned the responsibility of taking it down to the sisters. It's not that I minded. I was hoping to get a glimpse inside the house to see if it was really as bad as it smelled.

Ms. Gloria came to the door and invited me in. I stepped into the living room and immediately found it hard to breathe. Dozens of cats lounged on the couch, in every chair, on rugs, and stretched out on the hardwood floors. Apparently they weren't bothered by strangers, because none of them got up when I came in, they just turned their eyes to stare at me. It was a little disquieting, all those cat eyes staring at me like they were checking me out.

A fluffy calico was strutting across the kitchen table until Ms. Gloria saw me looking and snapped her fingers, "Get down from there!" The calico paid her no mind but curled up in the center of the table and stared at both of us.

"Where's Ms. Rita?" I asked.

"Oh." Ms. Gloria's face crumpled into a pile of pressed powder and red lipstick. "Didn't you know? Rita died six months ago."

"Oh." I stared into Ms. Gloria's thin blue eyes trying to think of something to say.

"It's all right." She relieved me of the need. "With her being in such pain and all it's better this way."

I agreed, wondering what kind of pain Ms. Rita was in that would make it better for her to be dead.

"I brought your mail." At that moment I noticed the envelope I held out to Ms. Gloria was from Rothner Funeral Home. Bills, I guessed.

Ms. Gloria nodded and I said, "I'd best be going now." She nodded again and opened the door.

I waited until I was safely hidden by the row of elderberry bushes before I bent over and put my hands on my knees, heaving deep breaths that cleared the cat hair out of my aching lungs. After that I was always especially kind to Ms. Gloria because of her loss. I could understand loss and that kind of made us sisters in a way.

I saw Ms. Gloria frequently at Hills Neighborhood Pharmacy. It was the only drugstore in town and it sold lots of things besides medicine. Every time Mitch, O'dell, or I, got a few coins together we'd walk down to Hills Pharmacy to buy something.

Sometimes Mr. Hill waited on us. He was a patient man with a kind face and a ready smile. He never seemed to tire of our questions, "How much is this?" or "How many pieces of that can I get for five cents?" He'd leave an adult customer waiting until we had made our choices and paid for our purchases.

Mr. Hill lost my patronage when it came to light that Mitch and O'dell had been stealing from him. The few times I saw Mr. Hill after that he always seemed sad, as if he knew something I didn't and it took the smile out of him.

Willy got an ear infection so Dad took me down to Mr. Hill's Pharmacy and told me to go in and pick up his prescription. A different clerk was at the cash register, someone I had never seen before.

"Where's Ms. Gloria?" I asked.

"Oh, didn't you know? She was murdered in her house."

Something inside me froze into a hard ball and plunged all the way to the floor. I stood there feeling empty, wordless, as I tried to fit my brain around the words I had just heard. Somehow I couldn't make myself think of Ms. Gloria dead.

"How? What happened?"

"Well," the clerk said, "one day a young man came into the store and started talking to Ms. Gloria. You know she never met a stranger." I nodded.

"He was real friendly and made a point of asking Ms. Gloria to help him pick out a perfume for his mother. She thought that was a right nice thing for him to do.

After a few weeks of coming in every day or so he came in looking real sad. He told Ms. Gloria that his mother had kicked him out of her house—said she had married a new husband who didn't want him around."

Mr. Hill came over just then and handed me Willy's prescription with a sad smile. I paid him two dollars and he walked back behind his prescription counter. The clerk continued:

"Ms. Gloria, being the kind soul she was, invited him to stay with her, just for a week or two, until he got it all sorted out and found himself a place to stay."

Another customer came in and bought some formula for their baby, paid the clerk, and left without saying much, so I waited. When the bell on the glass door jangled behind the customer, the clerk resumed her story.

"Ms. Gloria started coming in late to work. One day she showed up with a big purple bruise on her cheek. Mr. Hill wanted to take her to the doctor but she said it was nothing. She had bumped into a cabinet door she'd left open. Then one day, she didn't come to work. Now you know that's not like Ms. Gloria."

I nodded. That definitely wasn't like Ms. Gloria. She had been a fixture in Mr. Hill's Pharmacy for as long as I could remember.

"Mr. Hill tried to call her but no one answered the phone, so he went by to check on her. He knocked on the door for a long while but no one came to answer it. He thought maybe she'd left town. She'd been acting real strange lately.

"When she didn't show up for work for the next four days, Mr. Hill went back out to her house and nearly banged the door in. That's when he noticed the horrible smell . . ."

"The cats," I said. "The cats smell awful."

"It wasn't the cats," the clerk said shortly, as if irritated that I'd interrupted her story.

"It was Ms. Gloria. She was dead in there and had been dead for days."

My hand flew to my mouth and I knew my eyes were like saucers in my face. I couldn't blink, couldn't say a word.

The clerk didn't seem to notice. "Some of the cats were dead, too. Some folk think they starved for water, but I think they just laid down and died with their mistress. Those cats loved Ms. Gloria an awful lot you know."

I nodded. I knew. How could I forget? I turned around and walked out the door without saying bye.

"What took you so long?" My father demanded.

"I . . ."

He didn't wait for an answer but floored the gas pedal and got us home as soon as he could. Willy had a high fever and that was the urgency of the moment.

Chapter 41

The Davenport family didn't do so well with animals. It seemed like every one we got either died or went crazy. That's why I didn't get too excited when we got Blazer, but I had to admit he was cute.

He weighed in at about forty pounds and was part everything. Part lab, part hound, and maybe part bull dog. He was creamy beige with short fur and a blaze of white over his nose. That's why we called him Blazer.

Someone offered him to us and we got to keep him because they said he was a good hunting dog. Uncle Don got his brother, whom he named Mutt, so Dad and Uncle Don decided we should take the dogs to the woods and try them out. We would take Uncle Don's car because there was room for both dogs in the trunk.

"Yup!" Dad said, just like I had seen Uncle Bob do with his hounds, and sure enough Blazer and Mutt hopped right into the trunk. Uncle Don slammed the lid shut and we took off for the woods. Mitch and O'dell seemed excited about the hunt, but I was just happy to be getting out of the house.

It went downhill from there. Both dogs seemed determined to follow rabbit trails. No self-respecting small-game hunter wants their dog to chase rabbits. We could kill rabbits without the need for a dog. They were everywhere.

We heard Mutt moving along the trail, barking like mad, then heard Uncle Don shout at him to shut up. Mutt yelped. Mitch and I looked at each other.

"Did he kick him?" I asked.

"I bet he did," Mitch growled, his eye brows pulling together over his nose. He stomped along after that, muttering to himself.

Then we heard Mutt take off again, howling and barking. "He's treed a coon for sure," I said. "Or at least a squirrel." That's when we heard the shotgun blast. Mutt shut up right in the middle of a yelp.

"What'd he do?" Mitch demanded.

"He probably shot him." Dad said.

"He'd shoot Mutt?" I was incredulous.

"I'm about ready to shoot this stupid mutt too if he keeps chasing rabbit trails," was Dad's answer.

Mitch and I exchanged a look of pure hatred. What kind of man shoots a dog just because he chases rabbits? We were relieved when we got back to the car and Blazer was still in one piece. Uncle Don came out of the woods alone and popped the trunk for Blazer. I think he and Dad were discussing euthanizing Blazer on the spot, so we got him in the trunk real quick and shut the lid.

I was secretly pleased when we opened the trunk at home and found Blazer had left a big pile of puke on the matt for Uncle

Don to clean up. Uncle Don swore and we hurried Blazer off to the backyard where Mitch and I laughed our heads off. O'dell was still too mad to laugh so he stomped into the house and practiced throwing his switchblade against his dresser drawer. I didn't blame him much.

Blazer seemed destined for a short and unhappy life. Some of the boys in the neighborhood took to pounding him with rocks and sticks when we weren't home. I came home from school one day to find a two inch gash on his head. I cleaned it and soaked it with warm water, but Blazer was never right after that. He started snapping at everyone who came by him. One day he snapped at Willy and that night he disappeared. I knew he had to go but I missed him.

I bolted out of there, certain I heard her laughing behind me. They were all laughing. I couldn't hear them, but I knew it all the same.

Chapter 42

Meanwhile, Mitch and O'dell kept practicing the fine art of stealing. They never stole another car, but they stole radios, bicycles, and merchandise from stores.

I had tried it one time. Thankfully, I was young enough to be afraid to do it again. I had gone into the neighborhood grocery with Suzy. She said, "I'll show you how to get ice cream any time you want without paying for it." I didn't really want to steal, but I did want ice cream.

"It's really easy," she said. "What you do is go over to the ice cream freezer when no one is looking and take out the ice cream bar you want. Drop it into your panties and walk around for a few minutes. Then go pay for something else, like a piece of penny candy, and get the heck out of there."

I walked past the ice cream freezer at least a dozen times or so, my heart pounding like a bass drum in my chest. What if I got caught? I liked Jim and Anne, the store owners, and it would be awfully embarrassing to get caught stealing from them. But if I didn't, Suzy would think I was a sissy and make fun of me. Besides, I never got ice cream, hardly ever anyway.

So I made one last trip by the ice cream freezer, looked both ways, and picked up an ice cream sandwich, my favorite, and dropped it into my panties. It felt like the cold seeped into my bones and made it hard to move. I worried that the bulge in my panties would show through the outline of my skirt. *Why did I ever agree to do this?* I wondered. *This is crazy. I'm going to get caught.*

I looked at Suzy, already checking out her penny candy and winced. I'd have to go up there. Go through the checkout line to make it look like I had a reason to be there. Oh no. Oh no. I kept thinking. I considered putting the ice cream back but it just didn't seem right to do that after it'd been in my panties, so I made my way up to the counter where Anne waited to check me out. I couldn't look at her.

"How are you today, Chelsey?" she said.

"Just fine," I muttered without looking up.

"How's your mother and dad?"

"They're good."

"Is Willy feeling better? I know he was real sick a few days back."

"Yeah, he's better now."

The line was backing up. Why did Anne keep talking to me? She was chattering like a bird. She'd never done that before. I felt the ice cream melting. Oh, my gosh! It was running down my leg.

I bolted out of there, certain I heard her laughing behind me. They were all laughing. I couldn't hear them but I knew it all the same.

That was the beginning and the end of my career as a thief. I had other vices. I would leave the stealing to my brothers.

It wasn't safe yet and I knew it. I sat on the couch across from Dad and listened to him build himself into a fury~

Chapter 43

One night I went to bed early, relieved that Mother and Dad seemed to have resolved their latest argument, at least momentarily. Tonight I'd get a good night's sleep.

I was awakened by a hand on my shoulder at about midnight. I was being shaken. I sat up with a sinking feeling of impending disaster. This time it was Mother waking me.

"What . . ."

"Dad's gone to get the boys."

"Where are they?" I felt myself go rigid with fear.

"They're out in the alley with a bunch of other boys. They must have snuck out after we were asleep, but they made so much noise yelling and hollering they woke him up."

About that time Dad came slamming in the door, shoving Mitch and O'dell in front of him. Next thing I know he was yanking his belt out. "What do you think you're doing out there with those hoodlums, running up and down the streets like that?"

"We were just riding bikes with 'em, Dad." Mitch's face was so pale every freckle stuck out in 3-D.

Mitch didn't say, "riding *our* bikes," because Dad wouldn't let any of us have a bike. He said they were too dangerous so none of us could have one.

"Yeah," O'dell backed him up. "We weren't doing anything wrong."

Dad ridiculed them. "We weren't doing anything wrong. You don't think it's wrong to disobey your parents and go running up and down the street at night like hoodlums?"

I stood over in the corner hoping against all odds that he'd just whip them and get over it so we could all go back to bed. He whipped them all right, and gave them a push off to bed. "Get in there," he said, "but you'd better not go to sleep before I do or I'll whip you again. You go waking me up like that, don't you think you're gonna go to sleep while I sit up and suffer for what you've done."

The boys went to bed but I didn't. It wasn't safe yet and I knew it. I sat on the couch across from Dad and listened to him build himself into a fury. Mother went back to bed and I fell asleep sitting there in the chair. Dad couldn't tolerate that. He was mad and he had no one but himself to take it out on.

I heard him pulling the boys back out of bed. "I told you not to go to sleep," he said. He grabbed their arms and pulled them into the living room where he pushed them onto the couch. He made them sit up all night and yelled at them every time he saw them close their eyes. The next day we went off to school and he went to bed and caught up on his sleep. I guess he figured he deserved it.

Chapter 44

Graduation was coming up so I started talking about college. Something deep down inside told me I was wasting my breath, but I didn't listen. "I think I'll go to Bible College," I told Dad. He was dead silent.

A few weeks before graduation, I tried again. "I've always wanted to be a missionary," I said. "I think I want to go to Central Bible College in Springfield, Missouri."

He turned and looked at me, that evil glint in his eye telling me he knew exactly what he was doing, "If you do, I guess I'll just have to take the kids out of school," he said. "I was counting on you coming into the business to help me now that you went back and finished your schooling."

I didn't say anything. I couldn't. My hopes wilted like a cut flower in the hot sun. I'd never get away now. If thought I could walk away and leave my siblings to get along the best they could, now I knew better. Our father was ruthless. He would do whatever he had to do to make me stay home or bring me back. It didn't matter. Either way I was ruined. So I did as he asked. I graduated without any fanfare, and prepared to take my real estate exam. Within a few months after graduation I had a real estate broker's license and was firmly entrenched in my father's business.

I continued to sit at my father's feet and watch TV every night, to hold his hand in church, and to lie on the bed and read to him. There was no longer an ounce of love or respect left in it. I did it to survive, pure and simple.

Chapter 45

I wasn't the only one who had contemplated killing our father. I learned many years later that most of my father's children had entertained the thought on occasion.

Dora and O'dell plotted his demise from the bottom rung of a ladder with him perched at the top shouting orders at them.

Dora said, "We could give the ladder a little push."

"It's pretty high," O'dell said. "Do you think it'll kill him?"

"I think so," Dora hesitated.

"But what if it doesn't?"

Dora remembers cold chills running through her at the thought. If they didn't kill him he would kill them. They abandoned the idea.

O'dell's solution was to run away at his earliest opportunity and join the army. Mitch went with him. They were shipped out to different places and finished growing up in the military.

• • •

Our beautiful fiberglass boat was aging gracefully. I missed Mitch and O'dell when we went out on the river. Seemed like something was always missing.

One hot summer day we decided to have a picnic on the sandbar and invited Grandpa Kelsey to go with us. So we had Dad, Mother, Grandpa, Suzanne, Dora, Willy and me all in the boat along with an ice chest full of sandwiches and pop on a big block of ice.

When Dad headed the boat out of the current, Dora looked at that cool water and decided to be the first in. She jumped out right in front of the boat.

All I could think of was the sixty-five horsepower Evinrude behind me and the swirling brown waters of the Arkansas River all around us. Dora'd jumped too soon. If the motor didn't get her I was certain the current would. I kept thinking about the cadaver that was pulled out of the river the day we first got our boat.

I had learned later that he was twenty-three and he drowned trying to rescue his girlfriend. She had floated out too far on an orange air-mattress and got caught in the current. When he saw it was sweeping her downstream and remembered that she couldn't swim, he swam out to save her. Before he reached her, an undertow got him and pulled him under. His girlfriend held on to the air-mattress and screamed and hollered until someone came along in a boat and rescued her.

It was too late for her boyfriend. The next time anyone saw him was three days later when a search-and-rescue team pulled him out of the Arkansas River. His body, so I heard, had been caught in some wire deep down under one of the pilings, miles away from the sandbar.

That's why I leaned over the front of the boat and grabbed Dora by the hair. I had to keep her out of the current and away from the propeller. After a second or so I felt the pressure of the water pulling on her, pulling her away from me.

At the same time, I realized we were gliding into the shallows and I couldn't know the depth of the water. I thought about the weight of the boat with all of us in it and that big chunk of ice in the cooler, and I let her go. Better to take her chances with the motor and the currents than to be ground to death between the sand and the boat.

No one said a word and I think we all stopped breathing. Then she popped up behind the boat. She was safely out of reach of the current, but had a scrape under her arm where the propeller hit her in the armpit as she slid under it.

I tried not to think of what would have happened if she had gone under the propeller before Dad shut it off. Dora thanked me for saving her life. I was still shaking hours later when Dad decided he wanted to swim across the river.

He had the idea that he should show his courage by swimming without a life-saving apparatus and I should hang on to one and swim behind him. That way I could save his life if an undertow got him. I wondered how a boat cushion could save him and me, too, but he expected me to go and no one said I shouldn't. I had a bitter taste in the back of my throat like you get sometimes when you throw up just a little bit and then swallow it back down.

I waded out on the sandbar and looked back, maybe for the last time ever. Mother was sitting on the sand pouring Coca-cola into cups and setting them out on the blanket beside the sandwiches. I didn't see a place for me or Dad, but then, I wasn't sure I'd need one.

About halfway across, Dad turned around and came back. He said I was swimming too slow and it took the challenge out of it. Everybody knows you can't swim as fast when you're holding onto a boat cushion, but I didn't care about that. I was just glad to get my feet back on solid ground.

Chapter 46

The days of taking the kids on walks and singing in nursing homes were gone. We seldom heard from Mitch and O'dell who were living their private lives. Even little Willy was growing up. Dad made me stop paying attention to him when he turned thirteen.

"He's too old for you to tuck into bed like that."

"I just tell him good night and say a prayer for him," I protested.

"I don't want any more of it!"

Willy didn't really need me to attend to him at that point, because Mother had stepped up her nurturing abilities with him. She'd fight our father tooth and nail for Willy, trading insults and waltzing right into a violent rage, which invariably led to Dad taking me off alone with him.

• • •

After I started working at the real estate office, Suzanne began taking up the care of the kids at home. One day, Dad came home from work and Suzanne wasn't there. He found out she was down the street visiting with a friend. That friend turned out to be a twenty-something man who was bent on seducing sixteen-year-old Suzanne.

I was terrified that Dad would kill her if he caught her down there, so I ran down to get her and brought her home. He had got the truth out of the younger ones by the time we got there and he was furious. He met us at the door and shoved her into the house.

"You slut. You no good . . ." He was so mad his face was red as hell-fire and his hands trembled.

Dora was over in the corner shaking so hard she could barely stand up.

"Don't hurt her, Dad. Please don't hurt her."

Dad pushed Suzanne down and she squirmed around, trying to get off the floor.

Dora told me later that she kept thinking about O'dell's pet snake and wondering if Dad would squash Suzanne's head like he did the snake.

Suzanne finally got away from him and dashed out the door, running for her life. Dad took after her. I did too, but for different reasons.

Dad hadn't got to beat her yet and he wasn't through. I was terrified she would fall into the hands of a predator and get raped or killed if she ran away. I guess I thought I could keep her from that at home.

I caught up with Suzanne first and grabbed her, trying to talk her into calming down and coming back home. She came home, but was mad as Hades and scared stiff.

Dad kept ranting and raving about what he was going to do to the man down the street. He claimed Suzanne had been raped and he was going to kill the rapist.

Suzanne said it didn't happen. Dad said, "Take her to the clinic and have them check her out. We'll find out if it happened or not."

I'm ashamed to say I tried to get the doctor to do a check on her. The doctor didn't even come in the room, but sent the nurse to say we just needed to believe her.

"If she said she wasn't raped," the nurse said, "then she wasn't raped."

That made Mother happy because she didn't want to put Suzanne through that kind of check-up at sixteen. I couldn't help but think about when I was thirteen and she was willing to put me through it without a second thought. But then, that was me and this was Suzanne.

I don't know why I wanted the doctor to check her out, knowing she wanted to be left alone. Maybe I wanted to put her rapist in jail, maybe I wanted to prove she hadn't been violated so Dad would stop stomping around hating everybody. Or maybe I was jealous of Suzanne because she was Mother's pick and I knew Mother wouldn't have taken up for me like she did for Suzanne.

Whatever it was, I went home feeling like a low down skunk who had raised a stink and made a fool out of myself in the process. When we got home, Dad took me for a ride and got over being mad at Suzanne. I no longer felt like a fool. I didn't feel anything at all.

When our day to day existence was loaded with all the misery it could bear, I knew what I had to do~

Chapter 47

I think Suzanne hit bottom the day she was caught down the street. She now credits me for coming for her and keeping her from being raped or seduced. She got into the youth group at church where she got the encouragement she needed to grow beyond our wildly dysfunctional home. She wanted to go on a mission trip and worked to raise the money to do it. She had most of the money raised, and had trained for her part in the outreach, when Dad decided she didn't need to go after all. He didn't tell Suzanne that, he just told me. Suzanne's trip and her joy in going provided him with the leverage to overcome my resistance for several months. If I didn't give him what he wanted, Suzanne would lose her trip and have to tell her youth group she couldn't go because she was being punished. It was all up to me.

Suzanne wasn't going to suffer the humiliation and disappointment of missing her mission trip and letting her youth group down because of me. I walked the thin line between putting him off as long as I could and giving in before it was too late to save the day for Suzanne. When our day-to-day existence was loaded with all the misery it could bear, I knew what I had to do. I went into the bathroom and beat my fists against my head, drug my nails across my skin, and screamed soundless words behind that locked door. Then I walked out, emptied of myself, a vacant shell yielded to his will.

Suzanne returned from the mission trip with more confidence and poise than ever before. She was a princess. Five-foot-eleven and model thin, she impressed no one more than me. I drove up behind her one day when she was walking home from school. She seemed to float more than walk. She was worth every ounce of suffering I endured for her sake, but she'd never know the cost. I'd never want her to know. She hadn't asked me to pay it. She'd have been appalled. But she was a princess and I was proud of her.

The next year, Suzanne announced she would be going to Central Bible College. She was determined to make something of her life. Her victory was my victory. Her success was my success. When it was time to go, I took my clothes out of the closet and let her go through them to pick the ones she wanted. She was, after all, going to be living on a college campus and she'd need to dress nice.

Once when Suzanne came home for a weekend, she asked me, "Chelsey, are you really doing what you wanted to do, I mean working in real estate with Mom and Dad?"

"Yes," I lied. But I thought about it a lot after that. Maybe someday I would have a choice. *When all the kids are grown and out of harm's way. Maybe, someday.*

Chapter 48

Willy, who by now preferred to be called Will, was in Junior High School. He went out for the football team and got on it. I was proud of him, but I knew what that would mean for me. It gave Dad a lot of leverage.

Will would never know how many times Dad threatened to make him miss practice over some minor misbehavior, or even miss a game. Do you know what it means to a young man in school to be on a football team and then have to miss the game because he is being punished at home? The disgrace would have been unbearable.

One day when Dad was enraged—not because of anything Will had done, but because he wasn't getting his way with me—he picked a fight with Will. It escalated, like it always did, and became violent. He picked up a chair and tried to bash it over Will's head. I got in the middle and grabbed the chair.

"All right. Okay, Dad. Put it down." He knew the meaning of my conciliatory tone of voice. I had given in. He put down the chair and we left the house. I don't remember where we went. I don't remember what we did. I'm glad I can block out some of the memories because I don't need them all to know what happened. I just need enough of them to help me understand why I did what I did and how I came to be Dad's property.

Chapter 49

Somehow I took it into my mind that Dad and Mother might get along if they got out of poverty. Mother wouldn't write so many hot checks and Dad would feel better about himself. So I plunged into the real estate business with all my might. At nineteen, I was the youngest real estate broker in Arkansas.

I started encouraging Dad to buy investment real estate. I went with him to get a commercial loan so he could buy foreclosures and flip them for a profit. Most people wouldn't talk to him, but they'd talk to me.

Once I found a house that was being foreclosed by the Veteran's Administration. I'd heard the house was owned by a Vietnam veteran who suffered from post-traumatic stress disorder. I had it on good authority that the veteran had chased at least one investor away by sitting on his roof and firing his shotgun in the air to warn him off. That didn't bother my brave Dad much—he drove me right up to the house and waited at the curb while I knocked on the door.

The veteran wasn't there anymore, but a neighbor told me that he lived a few blocks away. He'd moved in with his mother. Undaunted by this discovery, I knocked on his mother's door, which eventually led to me sitting down in her living room and telling him what I would pay for his interest in the property. He must have thought my offer was fair because he didn't shoot me. He was in the middle of a divorce, so I had to sit down with his wife separately, but I got it all done and ended up with a deed to the house.

• • •

After a couple of years of real estate successes, we moved into a lovely new house in an expensive neighborhood. The yard was over a half-acre and shaded by mature oaks that reached thirty feet into the clouds. A neighborhood association shared the cost of a nature area nearby where I could go and sit beside a running creek and listen to the sounds of water rushing through stones.

Hope began to rise up in me like a spring sunrise, fresh and new, and wonderful. Dad left me pretty much alone for a while and I thought poverty had been the cause of his dysfunction. Little did I know then that he was getting his consolation somewhere else, which would have been an answer to my prayers if it had lasted.

• • •

I was allowed to attend Sunday school as long as I went into the class with old people. That was okay by me because Sister Annie taught the class and sometimes Brother James joined her. I don't know what it was about them, but just being there—with them—made me feel like I was a normal person. They talked to me as if my opinions counted. Sister Annie sometimes asked me to sing for the class Christmas Party. She always told me afterwards that I had a lovely voice.

They say you model the man you want to marry after your daddy, whether you liked him or not. I modeled the man I wanted to marry after Brother James. He was quiet and tender-hearted, gentle and strong. He never got ruffled, at least that I could see, and I never heard an unkind word come out of his mouth.

Sister Annie told me, decades later, that my mother went to Pastor Farrow once and asked if he thought my daddy might be molesting me. She told him a few indications, but left out the really important ones—the evidence she saw with her own eyes. He said naw. There wasn't any way Dusty Mitchell O'dell Davenport would do a thing like that. She just ought to go home and submit to him like a woman is told to do in the Good Book and everything would be all right.

Apparently, Pastor Farrow thought the Good Book says for wives to obey their husbands, when the Good Book actually says wives should submit to their husbands—and that involves using your own mind and conscience, which, to my way of thinking, has nothing to do with blind obedience.

• • •

Pastor Farrow may have thought mother ought to obey her husband, but according to Sister Annie, Brother James thought different. What he had to say about Pastor Farrow's advice sounded more like something out of the mouth of a lion than a teddy bear. I didn't hear about it until decades later, and by that time Brother James wasn't worrying about it, he had already gone on to his eternal reward.

Sister Annie had tried to talk to me about what she suspected was my awful, agonizing, secret. She knew it was awful, because she was pretty sure what it was. She knew it was agonizing, because no matter how she tried to get me to talk about my terrible secret, I just couldn't do it.

Many years later, I asked Sister Annie, "Did you suspect what was happening to me?"

"Yes, Chelsey, I did," she said in her soft southern drawl, "I suspected, but you know, you just didn't talk about things like that back then, not unless someone told you it was happening to them, and you couldn't tell me."

"Then how did you know?"

"Well," she said, "when a young girl like you goes to the altar every week, crying her heart out and sobbing, you know something terrible is happening to her."

Like the shadow of the Almighty, it seemed to me that Sister Annie was always there, hovering over me, smiling, touching my arm, inviting me to be a part of the social activities of her class. I could count on her being there when I ran to the altar week after week, kneeling on the carpet behind me, her hand on my shoulder. "Cry it out, Chelsey," she'd say. "Just give it to God, honey."

If only I could have—given it to God, I mean. But He didn't want it any more than I did. It seemed to me that my life was meant to be used up taking care of everyone else as best I could, which wasn't all that good anyway, and as soon as my job was done I would be free to die—thrown away in the Arkansas River or crashed into a steep embankment like I'd fantasized a thousand times over. Someday, it would all be over and I would be out of there—one way or the other.

· · ·

Will had taken to running away by this time. Every time he left, I was terrified that he wouldn't come back home. His drug of choice was alcohol and he used it liberally. One day he came home falling-down drunk, and Dad went into one of his rages. Mother wrapped her arms around Will and drug him up the stairs to his bedroom.

"He's not drunk," mother said. "He's just tired. I just need to get him to bed."

Dad's words are not repeatable in good company, but he seemed mad enough to hurt someone. Mother got Will into bed and stayed with him, while Dad sat downstairs and stewed. When she decided to come down, he was right on top of her. I went to my room and hugged my arms across my stomach, trying to stop the spasm in my colon. I knew what was coming.

"Don't, Mother." I begged silently. "Don't use that taunting tone of voice, you know it riles him up more." Of course she didn't hear me and I heard her sarcasm and his rage through the thin walls. Will slept through it. Dad grabbed me and got out the door long before Will woke up.

When Will moved in with a friend, only Dora was left in the house with Dad, Mother, and me.

· · ·

I said Will moved in with a friend, but that's not exactly what happened. I thought Will had moved in with a friend. Only recently did I discover that Mother whisked him off to live with her parents out in "the country." I was astonished.

"How did you get by with that?" I asked. I would have expected another display of firearms and threats against my dear grandpa's life if any of my father's children were taken into my grandparent's care.

"I fought for him," mother said fiercely, oblivious to the hot tar she rained down on my head. I was glad she fought for Willy, glad he found peace and a place to finish growing up with loving grandparents, but I was also terribly, achingly, aware that she didn't do it for me—that she wouldn't have done it for me.

• • •

Dora was getting married! No more late night talks when she came in from dates, no more flashing the porch lights when her date kept her sitting in his car in the driveway too long. Dalton B. Taylor was a lucky man. I made sure he knew it, too. I watched over Dora like a mother hen and gratefully didn't know all the boundaries Dora and Dalton crossed until they were married and it was too late for me to gripe about it.

Dalton B. Taylor started dating my sister when they were both sixteen. Teenage sweethearts. If Dalton had known the names I called the other boys Dora dated, he would have been proud of the less offensive ones I called him. Bart was barf and Danny was, well I can't say it here, but I didn't like the way he treated her. When she played the devil in a church play and he kissed her behind the baptistry, I was fit to be tied.

"Don't you be kissing boys you aren't going to marry." I was an old maid trying to keep a young girl chaste. It wasn't too hard because Dora naturally leaned that direction. When a boy in college asked her to sleep with him, she thought he really meant sleep and spent the night in his bed, afraid to come in after curfew, and discovered years later the extreme frustration she brought to that poor young man who had no idea she didn't know what it meant to "sleep" with someone.

The first man Dora ever slept with was Dalton B. Taylor, and that wasn't until after they said "I do" loudly, and in a public place.

The day after the wedding, Dalton brought Dora by the house and put his hand up her shirt right in front of me, just because he could. I forgave him and he became my brother and my friend.

• • •

A person will do lots of crazy things to occupy their time when they aren't allowed to live "normal" lives. I developed the skill of ventriloquism. Eventually, I acquired a full-body puppet and started writing scripts. Dora and Dalton encouraged me and helped me stage a meeting at the nearest housing project, where I talked about God, love, truth, and faith. My puppets (by then I had several) talked to the kids and got some fun banter going with them. Their parents sat in the audience and laughed along with them.

I asked for a volunteer to come up and converse with Polly, my favorite "little girl" puppet. A cute nine-year-old boy with the biggest almond eyes I've ever seen came to the front and had a meaningful conversation with Polly. One of his friends snickered, and LeRoy got embarrassed. Polly never blinked when he stepped right up in her face and swore at her. I invited him to church and he came the next Sunday, along with twenty-six of his friends.

After that success, I decided to do a "kid's crusade" in a nearby community. The five nights of meetings were like heaven for me, with kids crowding up to the front afterward to make a statement of their faith and talk to Polly and her friends.

When the pastor's wife called me a few days later and asked my advice about a personal issue, my whole way of thinking about myself began to turn around. Thank you, whoever you are, the wonderful woman who treated me like a peer and a friend. Did you know what you were doing for me or were you really asking my advice because you needed it? Either way, you are a beautiful lady, and one that I will never forget.

• • •

With all this unexpected encouragement, I went about my role-playing as a real estate professional with greater joy. I had passed my real estate broker's test at nineteen and started working for my father in his real estate office. I helped him buy rental houses and get them repaired and rented. I didn't do it for the money for, as I may have said, in the thirteen years I worked for my father I never got paid.

One day, my extroverted personality bubbled up and flowed over down at city hall. A young inspector took note of it and copied down my phone number from the permit card. That evening, right when Dad was in the middle of a rage, he called me. When I went to the phone, I could only thank God that Dad wasn't in the room. He had taken to getting his gun out frequently and holding it pointed toward Mother, sometimes all night. Sometimes, he made me sit and watch. I'd have sat there even if he didn't make me so I could distract him if he meant to pull the trigger. I don't know if that is one of the nights when he became the lone gunman, but he was in the kind of mood that often preceded violence in one way or another.

"Hi," the voice on the phone was friendly. I remembered his face—handsome, tanned, and kind. I'd have liked him for sure.

"May I help you?"

"Yeah," he said. "It's Steve from the housing department."

When I didn't say anything—couldn't say anything—he went on.

"I took down your number and thought I'd see if we could go for a coke, or something."

"Please don't call me again." I knew I sounded desperate, but I was too terrified to care.

I couldn't believe this was happening. I had let down my guard, unwrapped my arms from around my midsection (their customary position), and communicated like a real person (and not that plastic automation that I commonly presented to the world), and now, for the first time in my life, a would-be suitor had dared to call my home—had dared to break into the stony walls of my constricted prison, had knocked on the door of my heart, and placed me in mortal danger.

"Oh, I'm sorry . . . " He hung up just as the room faded into a blanket of thick darkness. I grabbed the dresser and steadied myself. I couldn't pass out—not now. Dad might guess what happened. He knew the phone had rung. As soon as I could walk I went back downstairs.

"Who was it?"

"Oh, it was a sales call."

He looked at me suspiciously and then went on with his tirade. It was hours before I could stop the trembling that seemed to shake every bone in my body.

• • •

About a year before Dora's wedding, just after the project meeting and the kid's crusade, I screwed up my courage and took a stand. The last of my siblings was about to launch her own life, so the only person still in harm's way was my mother. I had a talk with her.

I gave her a chance to get out first. We both knew that whoever stayed in my father's house alone was in grave danger of never making it out alive.

That's why, right after Dora announced her intention of becoming a married woman, mother picked an argument (which wasn't too hard to do) with my father, wrapping it up with, "I want a divorce. I want out."

I'll never forget the scene. She was sitting on one couch in the sunken family room and he was on the other. I was standing on the next level up, in the kitchen. My heart was pumping fast. Then my father said something to the effect of: "You can leave, but you'd better not try to take my property."

Mother's eyes flashed fire. I couldn't see them from where I stood, but I could feel them in the very air I breathed. I thought by now that nothing either of my parents did could surprise me very much, but my mother's next words took the breath right out of my lungs.

"Oh? What have you and Chelsey been doing all these years?"

When I heard those words I knew, right then and there, that as far as my mother was concerned I was expendable. *Expendable. A means to an end.* I always had been. But I never thought she would sacrifice me publicly, trade my life for sympathy in the courts when she was finally done with me. I knew that she was always aware of what was happening to me, but I don't think I truly believed she had consciously acknowledged it—until that moment.

As soon as Dora's wedding was over, the divorce proceeded. Apparently mother never raised the issue of her husband's infidelity in court. Exposing her knowledge of the facts in an effort to get a better divorce settlement wouldn't likely have done her any favors with the judge, anyway.

Mother moved out and I stayed. Freedom was coming. My chains are gone, the song says, I've been set free. Well, not yet, but sunrise was coming. After my long dark night. I could see it coming.

• • •

I was counting the days as well, because for the first time since high school graduation, I saw an opportunity to break free. Hope, that ever present flicker of life, flamed once again in the darkness of my existence and resurrected a part of me that I thought was long dead.

I was feeling the freedom close at hand one day when I went down to the city offices to pull a building permit for work on one of our houses. I say "our" because Dad insisted on putting my name on the deeds. He told me clearly that none of the houses were really mine—my name was just on there for insurance protection in case Mother ever decided to divorce him. That way she'd get one third and he'd keep two thirds.

• • •

Dora's wedding was beautiful. Suzanne and I were bridesmaids. People said I looked lovely but I didn't feel lovely. I felt like a walking, talking cadaver, still swimming upstream like the body I'd seen pulled out of the river—frozen into the right position but no longer breathing, thinking, or feeling. Just swimming in an ocean of pain that threatened to spill over and spoil Dora's special day.

You'd think I could have left as soon as Dora and mother did, but my wily daddy had planned ahead. "I'm gonna kill that woman if she tries to take my property!" he was fond of saying.

Mother did her best to keep trouble brewing, moving just across town and taking up with one man after another in her enjoyment of sudden freedom. She told me how much fun she was having at the VFC dances and taking trips to California with her latest beau. I tried to be happy for her, but that was hard to do when I seemed to be the only deterrent to the violence with which she was so familiar.

My father took her sexual exploits personally and it was all I could do to keep him from taking his guns over to her house and carrying out his vengeance.

When the divorce was finalized, he finally let it go and stopped threatening to kill her. I think he was semi-happy with his settlement, which was considerably in his favor.

Chapter 50

Sometimes when life seems its bleakest, it's because the darkest hour has come and sunrise is just around the corner. After Dora left and Mother moved out, I started getting my affairs in order to leave my father's house. Even then, I wasn't sure I could really do it.

It had been assumed for as long as I could remember that I, the eldest daughter, would stay in my father's home and take care of him. I even had a role model to follow.

When I was a young teenager, some previously unknown relatives came to call. One of them was Dad's uncle, and the other two were Uncle's daughters. The spinster women were in their mid- to upper-twenties. Their virtues were extolled by my daddy and mother.

The story, as best I can recall, was that their mother died when the girls were in their mid-teens, leaving several younger siblings and Uncle behind. Both girls came alongside their dad to tend the farm and raise the kids. Unfortunately, Uncle required more than babysitting from the girls and both of them grew up meeting his other, less appropriate, needs. When Uncle came to Arkansas, they dutifully got jobs and supported dear old dad.

I don't remember the words that conveyed the message I am about to relate to you, but it was as clear as day to me that any dutiful daughter, any woman who was worth her salt, would certainly do as the cousins had done and take care of daddy until their dying day.

After a few years, however, the eldest of the two daughters met a good man at work and fell in love. She was in her forties, I believe, and had a quiet wedding. The younger of the two daughters stayed with Uncle and cooked, cleaned, and cared for him. She was held up to me as the very icon of mercy and grace.

Uncle's daughter would have surprised my much deluded father. She sensed my struggles and got all her courage together one day and said, "Chelsey, you don't have to stay, you know."

"But you did."

That's when I learned, as Paul Harvey used to say, the rest of the story. When Uncle's daughter was twenty-seven, she was at her lowest point of despair, but she had the advantage of having no longer any reason to live. Her siblings were all raised, the last one had recently married and moved off, and Uncle's daughter gave her daddy an ultimatum.

"If you touch me again, I will leave. I won't live with it any longer. But if you leave me alone, I will stay with you and take care of you, cook, clean, run your house. But don't ever touch me, like that, again."

Uncle, she said, told her he was going off to kill himself. She let him go. He came home when he got hungry, and she made dinner. He never touched her like that again and she spent her life taking care of him.

"Don't wait too long," the icon of mercy and grace said to me. "I waited too long. Please, don't you do it."

Something about that conversation, considering the source of it, set free in me. I could almost see it—a white bird, similar to a sea gull, wheeling upward into the sky, a flash of white on blue, wings spread, ascending, going, going, gone. The obligation to "stay with daddy and take care of him," vanished. *Thank you, dear sweet lady. Thank you, Uncle's daughter. You saved my life and gave me your blessing to go out and make something of it.*

The pull of freedom grew in me day by day, but there was unfinished business to be done. Yes, I knew what I had to do. If I could survive what must be done, I would be free.

• • •

I worked like a professional mediator to get my parents on speaking terms after all the divorce papers were signed and heaved a sigh of relief when they met for dinner and parted on relatively good terms. Mother was safer than she'd ever been and I was closer to freedom than I'd ever been. I was also closer to death. I began fighting back when my father tried to molest me—fighting evil with truth.

Breaking free from my father's control was like driving a runaway car down a steep mountain. I had been in the garage so long, I wasn't sure if I had what it took to navigate on my own. The "vehicle" of my life was banged up, broken down, and missing vital parts. I doubted I would make it down the mountain alive, but at least I'd die wonderfully, recklessly, free!

• • •

Submitting to a mad man who controls your body, mind, and soul when you are numbed up is humiliating, doing the same thing when you are coming out of a life-long coma is like the difference between stepping in front of a speeding train when you're sleep walking, and doing the same thing when you are wide awake.

• • •

"Come lay down by me," my father said in that whining voice I'd come to hate.

Like an obedient slave I came to his side, lying flat on my back in a pool of misery.

"You know how much I hate what you do to me, don't you?" There. I'd said it.

Silence. Frozen. Excruciating. Dangerous silence. Then, the explosion.

"What do you mean, you hate it!"

I am not afraid. Not now. I am empty. Hollow.

"You never said that before." Quietly spoken. Harsh. Cold. A warning.

In my head, I said, "And if I had, who would have had to pay for my truth? Who would have been beaten, pushed into walls, or killed? Which of my siblings would have been shoved into rebellion, or run away from your hateful words? And who would have stood up for me? Not my mother, or her family, or yours. Not the law, for it was the arm of the law that surrendered my brothers into your hands when they begged for the safety of prison. No, my fine, upstanding, father, I never said no to you before."

"I puked," I said. "When you touched me . . . like that, I went to the bathroom and threw up."

"You threw up." Disbelieving.

This was the end. I had found my voice and talked myself into the grave.

I nodded. Miserable. Doomed. Alone.

• • •

What my father did to me after I told him the truth, showed me what O'dell's snake must have felt when my father stomped him into the dust beneath his foot. My father's gun stayed out on the dresser, in plain sight and fully loaded after that.

I was beginning to understand the nature of the force that had bound me all those years—and it was absolutely, beyond doubt, rape.

When I was five-years-old, my father didn't need a gun to get what he wanted from me. A child's need for love, shelter, protection, and nurture is weapon enough to assure the perpetrator' demands are met. By the time I was thirteen, it took the constant threat of violence toward those I loved to keep me confined in my prison. When my loved ones all went away, the gun came out to stay. And there it was. I had known it all along. My father would do whatever it took to keep me in his clutches, and if nothing he could do would keep me there, he'd blow us both away.

• • •

A few days later, my father called me into his bedroom. Just as if nothing had ever happened, he said, "Come lay down with me."

I pretended not to hear.

"Aren't you going to come in here?"

I complied, lying there stiff, and hateful, and angry. I knew what I was going to say. He reached over to touch me.

"I wanted to kill you, you know. I tried to get up the courage . . ."

Now he was rigid, fixed in stone.

"What do you mean . . ."

"After you took me out on that road, in Newport."

For once my father had nothing to say.

"I wanted to shoot you. Every time we went hunting after that, I tried, but I couldn't do it."

"Get out of here!"

I went to my room and waited. I stayed up all night. He would come . . .

But he didn't come. I got ready for work the next morning and went to the real estate office. The silent, empty, real estate office. The real estate office where I had worked for the past thirteen years, paying bills, making calls, processing sales, and never got a dime for it. Not one solitary dime. Well, that was over.

• • •

I knew my time was short. I didn't know exactly why I was delaying my departure, but I couldn't bring myself to go. Everyone would know my shame when I left. My father might find me and kill me, even if I got away. Mother was still just across town and I thought about the risk to her. So I went to see her. I told her I was leaving and begged her not to flaunt her joy to my father. I figured she would be just as glad to see him miserable as she was glad to see me getting away.

The next call I made was to Brother James and Sister Annie. They welcomed me into their home and talked to me like it was the most usual thing in the world for me to be sitting in their living room, telling them I was about to leave Arkansas. No one could know, I told them, except them and my mother. I could feel their joy at my unexpected news. I don't think they could have been any happier if I'd told them I was leaving them a million dollars. I left their house with a warm feeling spreading over my insides. Brother James and Sister Annie thought I was doing the right thing.

I talked to our accountant and told her in strictest confidence that I would soon be leaving, but I didn't want my father to know it. She seemed to understand my need for privacy as she gripped my hand hard when I turned to leave her office. I asked a friend to help Dad out with some of his work and she was glad to oblige. I learned to write a résumé and sent it out to places that I thought might hire me, giving them a contact number that my father didn't know about. I started going to a special park where I could sit and think without anyone standing over my shoulder. That's where I grieved the death of my father, which I was sure would be soon. A man who can't answer his own phone or get himself out of bed until late afternoon wasn't likely to make it on his own. He'd threatened suicide before. He'd do it now. I was sure of it.

So in my mind, I buried my father right there in Stoler's park, North Little Rock, Arkansas. Dug the hole, put him in it and walked away. Unfortunately, he wasn't ready to be buried just yet, so he came up with a novel idea.

I came home from work and he was waiting for me.

"I know you're up to something," he said.

"What do you mean?" I asked.

"You think you are taking off on me, don't you? I told you I'll find you if you do and I'll kill you. You aren't going to walk out on me and get away with it."

I protested that he had it all wrong, but he had sensed the smell of freedom on me and he wasn't giving up.

"It's that stupid brother-in-law of yours putting notions in your head, isn't it?"

I shook my head. I could see where this was going.

"You think Dalton can protect you? That little wimp? You leave me and I'll go over there and kill him. You think I won't, you're crazy."

My father had just managed to extinguish the light at the end of my tunnel and left me completely in the dark. I slipped into a depression as deep as hell itself. I believed every word he said. I could just picture him killing Dora's husband. I could visualize her sitting by his dead body, rocking herself back and forth, "Why Dad? Why did you do it? He never did anything to you." Her tortured eyes haunted me and I found myself sitting up late every night in my room, praying, reading, thinking, and aching somewhere in the deep region of my heart. Physical pains seized my chest and spasms in my colon drew me double, yet the next morning I was ready to go at seven and out the door to work. I'd come home when he called me and try to ignore the loaded gun on his dresser while I went through my ritual before going to his bed.

Then one day the sun broke through the darkest veil of night and washed over me in waves. My steps lightened and my face broke into smiles. I had a lilt in my voice and joy in my eyes. My sister Dora told me that her husband had been transferred to Michigan and she was going to follow him in just two weeks.

I took her to the airport. As I watched the Delta jet break through the sky, I knew I would be close behind.

• • •

One day I came home from work, tiptoed to my room hoping to escape my father's notice. As I reached the hall that led to his room on the right and mine on the left, he grabbed me. He seemed convinced that I was about to flee, which, of course was true.

"You wanted to kill me, did you?" He grabbed my hair and slung me into the wall. That's when I saw the gun in his hand. He watched me like a snake with his gaze fixed on a lizard. He cocked his gun and began to bump it against my chest.

"You're leaving me."

"No, Dad," I lied.

He didn't believe me. I had waited too long. There would be no more chances. He watched my every move.

"I'm going to the bathroom," he said late that night.

"If you try to run, I will catch up with you and I'll kill you. You hear me? You'd better not try to run while I'm in here."

In the mind of a child, father is omnipotent, he is omnipresent, and he is omniscient. He sees all, knows all, and is everywhere at the same time. In a sentence, small children believe their father is god. When the child grows up with trauma, that childhood fantasy becomes truth to him. He has seen the proof of it, or thinks he has, and he has suffered because of it. If the trauma never ends, the child may remain convinced of a lie that will keep him locked into a prison of fear.

In nightmares yet to come, the terrors of a thousand nights would come wrapped up in the lie that nowhere on this earth could I escape the violence and venom of the man I called father. So, I did what I had to do to convince him. One more time. One more time the man who no longer deserved to be called my father would rape me. With his loaded gun on the table beside him, he would live his fantasy one more time—the delusion that I was complicit in his crimes against me. One last time I would pretend to go along with his charade. One last time and I would be out of there.

• • •

The next morning while he slept the day away, I went to Stoler's park for the last time. I said good-bye to the beautiful old rock building and giant cider wheel. I went to the office and called my sister Dora. I told her I was leaving and asked her not to judge me if our father took his own life because I had left.

Dora begged me to come to stay with her and Dalton until I could get my feet on the ground—catch my breath. I told her I would come. I had one last thing to do.

I went to the bank and drew one thousand dollars from my father's bank account. I called the pastor of the church I had attended since nine years old and asked to speak to him and his wife. I went to their home and told them my story.

And then I left. I got on a Delta Jet and broke through the clouds, leaving behind a lifetime of misery. My happiness bubbled up and mixed with a sadness I couldn't explain. Could I live with myself after all the sorrow, pain, and disgrace of the past?

I looked into the clear blue sky and answered, yes. I could and I would. My seatmate reached up and turned on the overhead light. His name was Tim and he was traveling to a convention for the United Methodist Church. By the time we reached Detroit he had asked for my phone number. I told him I didn't know it yet, so he gave me his card. "Please call me," he said. "I don't want to lose you."

I tucked his card in my purse and watched him leave for the baggage area. But that, my friend, is another story altogether.

Afterword

Taking a Closer Look at Long-Term Child Debilitation

Why did she stay so long? This is the question that has been asked, perhaps thousands of times, since the disclosure of kidnapping and incest in the case of Elisabeth Fritzl, an Austrian woman who was confined in her father's cellar for more than twenty-four years, and more recently, Jaycee Dugard of California. Both women were victims of sexual exploitation, one at the hands of her father and the other by an abductor who incorporated his victim into his delusional "family" and passed her off as his daughter. Jaycee's two children, fathered by her abductor, believed their mother was their sister until the traumatic cycle was broken and Jaycee found the courage to walk into a police station and disclose her identity, after eighteen years of victimization. Both cases are clearly crimes of violence and both are clearly incest.

Clarification of the word "incest" and its legal, clinical, and emotional implications may help us understand why some victims get stuck in their trauma for many years, or even decades.

The American Heritage Dictionary of the English Language defines incest as:

1. Sexual relations between persons who are so closely related that their marriage is illegal or forbidden by custom.

2. The statutory crime of sexual relations with such a near relative.

This definition is severely limited in its concept and outdated as well. Family relationships have altered in multiple significant ways since the origin of the word incest, which actually comes from two Latin words meaning, *impure* and *unchaste*. Would anyone in our enlightened society today really accuse the child who has been sexually violated of being "impure" or "unchaste"? The word "incest" came into our vocabulary back in the day when girls were considered second rate to men, simply on the basis of their gender. Women's feelings, needs, and value were subordinated to the needs, desires, and ambitions of men. Though our social values in American have changed drastically since those days, the residual effect of such thinking is clearly evident in the way we define and respond to the crime of incest.

A more accurate definition of the term incest is found in the clinical interpretation of the word as stated by Sue Blume, author of *Courage to Heal*:

> Incest, as both sexual abuse and abuse of power, is violence that does not require force...It is abuse because it does not take into consideration the needs or wishes of the child, rather meeting the needs of the 'caretaker' at the child's expense...incest can be seen as the imposition of sexually inappropriate acts, or acts with sexual overtones, by - or any use of a minor child to meet the sexual or sexual/emotional needs of one or more persons who derive authority through ongoing emotional bonding with that child. (Blume, 1990, p. 4)

Some key elements in the commission of incest are:

- Sexual exploitation of the child by someone in a position of authority over him or her
- Seducing the child—introducing him or her to carnal knowledge that entices a sexual response from the child and then blaming the child for responding.
- Violation of the balance of power, the child cannot simply walk away
- Violation of the child's trust
- The perpetrator exploits the child's dependency upon him (or her) for essential physical and/or emotional needs
- The perpetrator has perceived control over the safety of the child and/or others whom they love
- The perpetrator has perceived influence or control over shaming or disgracing the child and/or causing the child to be rejected or abandoned
- The child believes he or she may be the cause of the breakdown of the family if resistance or disclosure occurs
- Often, the only source of affirmation and attention may be the perpetrator who exploits the child's natural needs by sexualizing the relationship.
- An absorption by the perpetrator of the victim's emotional energy, inappropriate expectations that place "adult" responsibilities on the child, and/or making the child feel responsible to meet the physical, mental, or emotional needs of the adult.

In recent months we have seen an increase in the number of disclosures by victims of long-term sexual victimization. Most of the victims were women, though we should not overlook the trauma of life-long captivity experienced by Elisabeth Fritzl's children, including her sons. While they may not have been sexually exploited, these boys and others who experience similar trauma have suffered debilitating abuse, abandonment and severe neglect as well.

One courageous young man who has spoken up about his abduction experience is Shawn Hornbeck. He was 11 when he was abducted near his Richwoods, Mo., home in 2002 and spent four years in captivity. Hornbeck, now 18 and in high school, told People Magazine (September 2009) that psychotherapy was a key element to healing. "One of the things that helped me is that we talked about how I could better myself from what happened, how I could use those terrible, awful experiences," he says. "I know it sounds crazy, but those experiences have made me a better person."

Like Jaycee Dugard, Hornbeck had a certain amount of freedom and faced questions after he was freed about why he didn't escape his captor. "You're brainwashed. It's as simple as that," Shawn says. "It's like you are on autopilot, only someone else is controlling all the switches. They control every little, minute detail in your life. Everything."

That control may be reinforced by terror, by manipulation of a child's basic needs, and/or by physical force. Either way, when the child sees no way of escape he or she will adapt to the most horrendous environment in order to survive. When asked why Jaycee Dugard stayed so long, Emie Allen of the National Center for Missing and Exploited Children replied: "Many kidnap victims of any age bond with the people who abduct them. It's very difficult for any human being to be angry and desperate year after year . . . "

Children who bond to the perpetrator who sexually exploits them, whether they are in that position because of an abduction or through family relationships, are victims of an insidious interference of the child's ability to develop psychologically, emotionally, socially and even biologically. There is mounting evidence that ongoing trauma interferes with brain development and may permanently alter the way a survivor's brain functions.

Some professionals have suggested that the Stockholm Syndrome may be responsible for the bonding some victims experience with their abductor. This syndrome occurs when someone is abducted or terrorized without any possibility of escape readily available. In order to survive, some victims misinterpret the abductor's self-serving behaviors (such as feeding them or allowing them to go to the bathroom while still maintaining control over them) as kindness. In such cases, the victim may bond to the abductor and even begin to resent those who did not come to their rescue, perceiving them as their enemy, feeling that their loved ones or law enforcement officials have failed them.

Children who are taken hostage (physically, psychologically, and emotionally) by a family member are in a similar position, however, they may experience a deeper level of despair because of the violation of trust, abandonment by the non-perpetrating parent, and a sense of family loyalty that makes it almost impossible for them to tell. Keeping the secret is considered by some therapists to be the most damaging of all aspects of inter-family sexual abuse.

When asked for his insights pertaining to the Jaycee Dugard abduction and long-term confinement, Psychiatrist, Dr. Keith Ablow, made the following observation:

While I am not treating Jaycee Dugard, I have helped hundreds of people take this journey. Because her story—while far more dramatic—is a cousin to every story of an abused girl or boy who clings to parents who are that only in name and not in deed, parents who erode self-esteem by inflicting emotional or physical suffering on their offspring. These children, like Ms. Dugard, fear they will be abandoned or that they are unlovable and they ally with their "captors," too. Only from the relative safety of adulthood, in a healing and therapeutic relationship, are they able to admit the terrible truth that what they took for love all through childhood was never that, and that finding what they need in the world will mean seeing what was unfairly denied them. Stockholm syndrome, it turns out, is far more common than most people think. It doesn't take a bank robbery or an abduction to trigger it. It happens in many, many "homes" that are that only in name.

Dr. Ablow is absolutely right. Whether a child is victimized by a family member or violently abducted from her home and raped by a stranger, many of the core dynamics that affect the survivor are the same.

Another component involved in severe cases of child debilitation, is the effect of ongoing trauma. Remember the experiments by Dr. Martin E.P. Seligman that resulted in his theory of learned helplessness? His theory (based on experiments with dogs) explains that once a human being learns that it is impossible to escape from a traumatic event or environment, they may adapt to the environment they are in and be psychologically unable to remove themselves from it even when the original debilitating event ceases.

While this theory provides a great deal of insight into why people who are severely traumatized over a long period of time may give up, it is limited in the aspect that people are, fortunately, made from "a different mold" than dogs and have spiritual, mental, and emotional resources that may enable them, at some point in time, to recover their ability to choose, act on their strengths as a survivor, and take a courageous step into freedom. With support of loved ones, the wisdom of therapy, and the help of a Power higher than themselves, they may learn that they are not helpless after all and begin to change and grow, making good use of the strengths that they developed in order to survive.

One other biological aspect of the debilitating nature of ongoing trauma concerns the victim's "flight or flee" stress response. What happens when that response is repeatedly triggered, but the victim is too terrified to do either? What happens if he or she has learned as a child that an attempt at either is futile, or is so dangerous that any effort to escape must be avoided? What if he or she believes that any attempt to break free will result in bodily harm to him or herself or loved ones? In time, the victim may go into the third response to perceived threats. He or she may become "frozen," unable to function beyond the level of bare necessity and become locked into the traumatic cycle for many years to come, or even decades.

As our society learns to place the blame entirely on the perpetrator of incest, and respond with compassion and understanding to the victim, the emerging survivor will begin to regain her or his dignity and confidence. I propose that we eliminate the use of the word "incest" entirely from our vocabulary.

The word "incest" feels the same to some survivors of sexual violation that the obscenity "nigger" feels to a black person. The word is offensive and inappropriate. Just as people of a minority race whose skin is dark do not deserve to be labeled by an obscenity, so victims of sexual violation are not unchaste or impure because of the crimes committed against them as the term implies. Who wants to come forward and ask for help when doing so requires that they acknowledge the very thing they are most afraid of—that they will be considered dirty, damaged, and less than normal? The word "incest" focuses on the sexual aspect of the crime and fails to address other debilitating components of the crime, such as abandonment by other caregivers, severe physical or emotional neglect, other forms of abuse such as terrorizing, physical, psychological, and/or emotional abuse that are almost always present to some extent, and the frequent lack of an adequate support system.

I believe it is possible for us, as a society, to remove a tremendous burden of shame from the shoulders of debilitated children and adult survivors if we cease to use the word "incest" and properly label their experience as "Child Debilitation," for that is exactly what "incest" does to a child. It debilitates them. On some level, for a certain period of time, the child is unable to stop the trauma and live a normal life. Let's remove the stigma of "unchaste" and "impure" from our vocabulary and restore dignity to those who have been debilitated by the synergistic effects of sexual violation, multiple forms of abuse, abandonment, and severe neglect.

You may be asking, how can we help children caught in the tangled web of an abusive family system? We should develop a consistent protocol for inter-family responsibility that would provide education and support for the non-perpetrating parent, providing opportunities for the child to disclose the abuse without fear of retribution or abandonment by other family members. Adults can be equipped to recognize and intervene on behalf of the child through training such as the *Darkness2Light* program, *Stewards of Children,* which can be offered to teachers, churches, corporations, and individual families.

Children can be empowered through age appropriate education such as "Good touch-bad touch," programs. Parents can talk to their children about abuse and teach them how to help their young friends disclose "family secrets" in a safe manner. This is particularly important because children who are afraid to disclose abuse to adults will sometimes confide in a peer. For more information about age appropriate training in this area you can go to our website at www.Child-Debilitation-Syndrome.com.

One last note, if a biological disease was rampant in our society that severely affected the development of 25–30% of our children, resulting in serious mental, emotional, and physical disorders throughout their lifetime, we would react with haste and passion to subdue that disease and deliver our children. Yet, we all know that sexual abuse affects between 28–38% of girls and more than 20% of boys. Studies show that 80–90% of sexual abuse is perpetrated by someone the child knows and trusts, and 30–40 % is perpetrated by a family member. Only about 10% is perpetrated by a stranger.

Clearly, the horrors of debilitating abuse, with its counterparts of abandonment, and severe neglect, reside primarily in the home. If we want to save the children, we must make parents accountable for the protection of their own children and hold them responsible when they violate that sacred trust. We need to go into the schools, corporations, and churches in

America bearing the banner of truth about child debilitation and we need to STOP it.

- Sound the alarm---talk about child abuse to others
- Train parents and care-givers,
- Offer compassionate assistance, and
- Protect our children.

For more information go to our website: www.Child-Debilitation-Syndrome.com We welcome your suggestions and constructive ideas about how we can help STOP abuse and protect our children. We'd love to hear from you.

Did You Know?

Father-daughter and stepfather-daughter incest is most commonly reported, with most of the remaining reports consisting of mother/stepmother-daughter/son incest. Prevalence of parental child sexual abuse is difficult to assess due to secrecy and privacy; some estimates show 20 million Americans have been victimized by parent incest as children (Jeffrey Turner, 1996).

One researcher describes incest as: " . . . the sexual abuse of a child by a relative or other person in a position of trust and authority over the child. It is a violation of the child where he or she lives—literally and metaphorically. A child molested by a stranger can run home for help and comfort. A victim of incest cannot" (Vanderbilt, 1992, p. 51).

Incest traditionally describes sexual abuse in which the perpetrator and victim are related by blood. However, incest can also refer to cases where the perpetrator and victim are emotionally connected (Crnich & Crnich, 1992).

"Intra-family perpetrators constitute from one-third to one-half of all perpetrators against girls and only about one-tenth to one-fifth of all perpetrators against boys. There is no question that intra-family abuse is more likely to go on over a longer period of time and in some of its forms, particularly parent-child abuse, has been shown to have more serious consequences" (Finkelhor, 1994).

In the adult retrospective study, victimization was reported by 27 percent of the women and 16 percent of the men. The median age for the occurrence of reported abuse was 9.9 for boys and 9.6 for girls. Victimization occurred before age eight for 22 percent of boys and for 23 percent of girls. Most of the abuse of both boys and girls was by offenders 10 or more years older than their victims. Girls were more likely than boys to disclose the abuse. Forty-two percent of the women and thirty-three percent of the men reported never having disclosed the experience to anyone. (Source: Finkelhor et al., 1990.)

Links for more information about biological damage to the brain caused by childhood trauma:

- http://www.lawandpsychiatry.com/html/hippocampus.htm
- http://www.lawandpsychiatry.com/html/PTSD%20Memory%20and%20Brain2.pdf

Resources

24/7 Hotlines and Crisis Services
Suicide Hotline
1-800-SUICIDE
1-800-784-2433

American Humane
National Domestic Violence Hotline
www.ndvh.org
1-800-799-SAFE (7233)

CHILDHELP/IOF Foresters
National Child Abuse Hotline
1-800-4-A-CHILD
(TDD) 1-800-2-A-CHILD
Provides multilingual crisis intervention and professional counseling on child abuse. Gives referrals to local social service groups offering counseling on child abuse. Has literature on child abuse in English and Spanish. Operates 24 hours.

CONFIDENTIAL Runaway Hotline:
800-231-6946

National Youth Crisis Hotline
800-442-HOPE (4673)
Responds to youth dealing with pregnancy, molestation, suicide, and child abuse.

Covenant House Nineline
www.covenanthouse.org/programs_nl.html
1-800-999-9999
Help, support, and caring are provided immediately to every Nineline caller. For the child lost in the pain and confusion of growing up, a listening ear can help by providing support and guidance. For the abused child a call to the Nineline can begin the process that will provide safety for that child Kids and parents can reach out any time of the day or night for free, confidential, and immediate crisis intervention by ialing

Darkness to Light
www.darkness2light.org
1-866-FOR LIGHT
1-866-367-5444

Prevent Child Abuse America
www.preventchildabuse.org
312 663-3520
Toll-free: 1-800-244-5373

National Council on Child Abuse & Family Violence
www.nccafv.org
202 429-6695

National Center for Victims of Crime
www.ncvc.org
Toll-free Helpline: 1-800-FYI-CALL

RAINN—Rape Abuse and Incest National Network
www.rainn.org
1-800-656-HOPE
1-800-656-4673

Survivors of Incest Anonymous
www.siawso.org
World Service Office
410-893-3322